Across the Years by Rail

Across the Years by Rail

A Random Recall of
Trains and Scenes of Yesterday
and Engines that Steam no More

by

W.H. Macleod

First published in 1998 by
The Pentland Press Ltd.
1 Hutton Close
South Church
Bishop Auckland
Durham

British Library Cataloguing in Publication Data.
A catalogue record for this book is available
from the British Library.

ISBN 1 85821 566 8

Typeset by George Wishart & Associates, Whitley Bay.
Printed and bound by Bookcraft Ltd., Bath.

This book is dedicated to:

1 A host of workmates; tutors; trainers and associates, across the wide realm of locomotive and mechanical engineering (many no longer with us), who unstintingly shared and imparted their knowledge, skills, enthusiasm and companionship and to whom adequate thanks were never given but whom the writer would have dearly loved to have thanked individually.

2 Head Teacher Mrs Jean Kemp of Guardbridge School, who believed that the glimpsed contents of the writer's memoirs including the following pages were worthy of a wider readership and who first instilled the 'preposterous' notion of publication.

3 My wife, Betty, for tolerating the hours spent on these pages that should have been devoted to demanding domestic matters. Also for valuable assistance with proof checking.

CONTENTS

List of Illustrations

CHAPTER 1

A railway enthusiasm and its possible origins

Why had railways fascinated me from an early age?

This was a question that I had oftentimes pondered and it is highly probable that an identical analysis has been conducted by many others who have found in Railway Operation the same compulsive interest and, from that source, derived lasting pleasure. As mentioned earlier in my memoirs, at a relatively tender age I had been given, by a great-aunt, a children's book on railways by Cecil J. Allen. Perhaps that kindled the first spark, which was fanned to flame by other publications such as an early edition of the *Children's Encyclopaedia*.

Another major influence arose from early rail travels. My aunt had married a shipmaster and on his retiral from a lifetime on the world's oceans, they had set up house in Tayport in 1927. To this location, from that date, I became a regular traveller with at least one annual pilgrimage in my early years. Indeed, from around the age of five or six, I spent a summer holiday of at least one week's duration with them every year, a practice that continued until the nineteen forties.

The location of their house was superb, for not only did it command a matchless view of the River Tay and all its shipping, but directly in front of that house there ran the single-line railway from Tayport to Dundee via the Tay Bridge.

This was, in actuality, the loop line from Leuchars Junction to Dundee. Prior to the building of the first Tay Bridge the line had terminated at Ferryport on Craig, which was renamed Tayport by the railway company; and from there wagons were taken on the world's first (steam) train ferry to Broughty Ferry across the

1. Tayport: site of early railway viewing. Rail trackbed atop embankment can be seen between house and river. (Photo: A.M. Macleod, c.1949)

Firth of Tay and thence to Dundee by rail. On construction of the Tay Bridge, a direct line was constructed between Leuchars Junction and the new bridge and a branch line run from Tayport to the bridge. Between the fall of Bouch's bridge and the completion of its replacement Barlow bridge, the train ferry was temporarily reinstated.

A locomotive pageant: tank engines and Driver Pearson

The greatest intensity of traffic on the branch was generated by the Tayport to Dundee local service, which conveyed the Tayside commuters of their day from the Fife stations of Tayport, East and West Newport and Wormit to Dundee (Tay Bridge Station). This was a service of remarkable frequency which as late as 1939 saw the first and last trains from Dundee at 6.50 a.m. and 9.56 p.m. (10.44 p.m. on Saturday) respectively and from Tayport at 6.22 a.m. and 10.25 p.m. respectively.

Interlarded with these trains, however, were Thornton to

Dundee trains coming round the East Neuk of Fife (with counterparts in the reverse direction). Additionally there was a small, residual service of 'through' trains to Edinburgh from Dundee and, in reverse, from Dundee to Edinburgh.

Freight traffic on the Tayport/Wormit section was negligible (although there were significant freight movements between Leuchars Junction and Tayport, conveying esparto grass from Tayport to Guardbridge; coke and moulding sand to Tayport Foundry from the south; and timber from Tayport harbour to the sawmill. The rail-connected spinning mill also relied entirely on rail-borne freight for many a day.

2. Tayport harbour, with trawler leaving, possibly after coaling: a regular practice. (Valentine postcard, early 20th century)

Until the war, the Dundee trawlers were coaled at Tayport and coal had to be hauled from the south. The extensive lyes witnessed the heavy merchandise of earlier days. Some light engine movements also occurred of a late morning and in early evening (which can be seen in a later essay in borrowed-camera photography, in which the object is the Scott Class locomotive 'Dirk Hatteraick', obviously demoted by then from main-line duties and idling on this ramification of sidings after a trip working from Leuchars).

There was, therefore, a grand parade of engines to be seen daily. In the hours of darkness the sight was of a pyrotechnic nature, as the locomotives climbed hard from the platform extremity at Tayport station for some two miles. On a winter's night this was quite spectacular and the engine barks heralded, from afar, the oncoming spectacle and summoned a child spectator to a window seat. The blasts were all the more dramatic as the initial part of the climb was confined in a narrow rock cutting, and the whole region seemed to reverberate as the rocky walls threw back their echoes.

One got to know the rudiments of the timetable, and certain trains provided salient features in the daily round of events. Amongst these were those at 10.01 a.m., 1.13 p.m. and 8.07 p.m. to Dundee, whilst the 9.36 a.m., 12.56 p.m. and 2.35 p.m. from Dundee were likewise regarded, since these were 'through' trains and as such were used by the family, from time to time, to enter or exit that blessed spot. Through trains were more interesting as they might be hauled by more exotic engines (i.e. engines other than the habitual, though well-loved, branch line engines).

One engine claimed my unswerving interest, in that misty region before any organised system of viewing had commenced. This was Black Duncan whose ten o'clock bark would be awaited with total anticipation and, strategically seated before the dining room window, I would watch with joy as her smokebox emerged from the screening whins of the West Common and she steamed forward over the tiny overbridge and ascended the long grade past the lesser lighthouse; to disappear from view by the quarry road, where rose 'the distant' for Tayport North.

In years to come, I would acquire a deep attachment for the daily local performers 9440 and 9445: the C16 superheated tank engines of W.P. Reid's design, whose profile I considered most pleasing to the eye. These seemed to 'emerge', however, in later years. In my early state of locomotive illiteracy, I could not identify in a positive manner the small tank engines handling this duty, but even then, they seemed to such an uninitiated eye to have something of the archaic in their appearance: but, then, they *were* most assuredly different in that they carried their safety valves on the dome.

3. C16 Class engine as used intensively on Dundee commuter trains, seen in BR livery. In this case at Arbroath. NBR Class 'L', designed by W.P. Reid and built by NB Loco Co., February 1921. Tractive effort: 19,078 lb. (Photo: Author, 20.7.51)

One vision drifts from some half remembered recollection of these far-off days.

It is an afternoon of monstrously heavy rain. I climb, with a relative, the steep flank of the little track that ascended to Commonty Road, abreast of the point where the deep cutting gives way to embankment. A straining engine emerges bunker-first with steam streaming from her dome-top safety valves, which diffuses into the incessant rain that seems to sheet down her side tanks.

Just one facet of an isolated memory encapsulated in time. What was she? I have oft-time wondered. A Drummond-designed 4-4-0 Tank perhaps?

There is no lack of detail in the C16 tank memories, and another abysmal attempt at locomotive photography was inevitably applied to one such, in the south dock at Leuchars Junction where she rested after bringing in the St Andrews local. It is of old 9445 herself – the object of much admiration. Perhaps she was Driver Pearson's engine: he was a portly man whom I recall having had identified in later childhood. A recollection of her gave pleasure to a student of genealogy, who (by one of those weird coincidences that we encounter from time to time) chanced to sit next me in Cupar library one afternoon around 1994 as I was studying an old parish register.

Was I seriously interested in family history? he enquired. He himself was deeply interested, he said, and gave advice on routes and sources to follow. Tayport was mentioned as one of his current research locations.

4. C16 Class engine about to leave Tayport for Dundee, footplatemen and guard in attendance. The old 9445 in a new garb. Built by NB Loco Co. in 1916 and withdrawn 1961 (Photo: Author c.1949/50)

I half-heard the name Pearson and my thoughts drifted back to that old C16, climbing the branch or performing the train reversal that I had so often watched with fascination in those golden days of youth.

It all came out and he was enthralled when I was able to recall 'his Uncle Davy' in command of 9445 and follow it up with the salient features of this object of my youthful admiration. Astonishment is not a sufficiently powerful noun to describe his amazement.

I in turn was transported in a twinkling from current mundane existence to re-catch the enthusiasm and optimism of those distant days.

Early locomotive sightings on the Tayport branch

How broad was the range of engines that one could observe from that most perfect of all grandstands! Though the majority were of NBR lineage, and route availability precluded the heavy modern LNER locomotives, Gresley's modified Director class were frequently observed with all their evocative names: 'James Fitzjames'; 'Ellen Douglas' and 'Baillie Macwheeble' to name but a few. Of the Scott Class, there steamed past not a few: 'Black Duncan'; 'Simon Glover'; 'Peter Poundtext' and a great host of others.

'Glens' were not less represented: 'Glen Cona'; 'Glen Dessary'; 'Glen Beasdale' and 'Glen Quoich' were just some of the Glens of the West recalled.

Intermediates would appear and the Occasional J36.

On a Sunday, while the C16 'tanks' had their weekend servicing, J37s would stand in. The late morning light engine could be an ex-NER J21 (ex duties on the Carmylie light railway?).

In the very early days, the branch-line 'tanks' were noted – even then – as being 'different'. Their safety valves were dome-mounted and they seemed to an untutored eye to be somehow small and compact engines (4-4-0 NBR Tanks, which became

LNER class D51, the last of which were withdrawn in 1933, perhaps?). After their going, the well-proportioned C16 4-4-2 'tanks' ruled for many a day (9440 and 94445 the usual stalwarts and much admired).

But if LNER Pacifics could not be seen at forty feet, they could be viewed some two miles away across the river, where ran in full view by West Ferry, the main LNE line to Aberdeen via Arbroath, Montrose and Kinnaber Junction (from historic racing days recalled). That artery was a joint line (LNE/LMS), the latter servicing Broughty to Arbroath as well as Forfar via Barnhill (with the possibility of access to Kirriemuir on its branch beyond that county town).

My uncle regularly used a superb pair of Zeiss binoculars (from a Great War German submarine) to scan the intense river traffic and these I was allowed to use. Through their lenses, I was to scrutinise Gresley's mighty locos and – all unknowing – NBR Atlantics, as well as diminutive 0-4-4 Caley Tanks and many another more exotic engine than the Tayport Branch could rise to.

CHAPTER 2

An annual rail pilgrimage

The annual pilgrimage to Tayport is fondly remembered, though recollections of the very early journeys are now of a more time-worn texture, with certain dominant features retaining their original hues whilst adjacent sections have faded and others – in part – have well nigh vanished. Oft I have sought to recapture the missing remnants but alas, if they exist at all they – computer-wise – are in some directory the access to which is either unknown or beyond residual powers of definitively-limited capability. What I refer to are events taking place during the years 1927 to 1933 or thereabouts.

5. Exterior of Sinclairtown station (2nd station) of North British Railway. A works outing seems to be about to entrain. (Thos. McLaren's Linen Works, Kirkcaldy). Note Kirkcaldy tramcar in St Clair St. (Photo from author's collection c.1912–16)

The pattern of the annual journey was impressively regular, as if decreed by the rites of the Medes and the Persians of Biblical times. I was taken by another aunt, who was a sister of my married aunt and of my father, whom I (and, when he became of an eligible age, my younger brother) joined on her summer stay at Tayport. My father (in like fashion to his contemporaries in Scottish industry) got only the 'Trades week', as a summer break and, thus, I was much more fortunate than many of my class-mates and acquaintances in having a double summer holiday.

The journey was inevitably made in mid week and, with equal certitude, commenced at Sinclairtown Station. The selected train was invariably the 11.28 a.m. from that point – a timing which seemed to remain inviolate across the years. Non corridor stock is recalled as the selected carriages, and as the years progressed, I seemed to note that the engine was almost always No. 9885 (which many years later I was to identify as an Intermediate of NBR design).

Sinclairtown Station was a curious place. The booking hall and office were built on a bridge above the tracks which was contiguous and parallel with the bridge that carried St Clair Street. The booking hall was relatively spacious and the entrance from the street generous. Access to the tracks was by means of two stairways, one on either side of the tracks, which were entered from a corridor which abutted the station offices and was in effect an enclosed footbridge with glazed front (possibly cantilevered off the main structure).

The inclined walls of the access stairways were likewise glazed. A goods lift was positioned at each end of the corridor, but this was located in a mysterious alcove from which region passengers were discouraged. The lower exits gave on to narrow platform extensions which penetrated the dingy tunnel structure formed by the station administrative and booking regions above and the roadway beyond, and were not generally approached by the travelling public. All of these regions were pervaded by a slightly acrid and indubitably sulphurous aroma of locomotive smoke which, no doubt, seeped upward and outward from the tunnel-like confines beneath as a token of recently-departed traffic.

Both north and south platforms boasted a waiting room in typical railway structural form, with their projecting awnings suitably decorated with unmistakable convoluted railway fretwork.

At the 'northern' end of the northbound (down) platform rose a signal mast carrying the Sinclairtown outer home and the Dysart distant signals against a background of the masonry forming the abutment of the Church Street over-bridge. At the times of our morning travel the station was seldom busy but such was not the case at departure times of popular (and especially Saturday) Edinburgh trains and those likewise returning from the capital.

Sinclairtown, a vanished station: booking office routines

The booking office was an equally mysterious establishment which travellers normally only saw through the severely limited orifice of the booking window, a semicircular opening in the timber faced wall with a projecting wooden shelf on to which the tickets eventually emerged. Inside the window could be discerned the iron base of the franking unit into which the booking clerk inserted the tickets in turn and from which the little pale green tickets emerged after the inevitable 'clonk clonk' of the stamp as it effected its esoteric machinations. In the inner recesses of this sanctum the railway telegraph needle could be heard sending out its continuous chatter.

To whom did it 'speak'? What dire or routine messages did it faithfully transmit? The slave of the ticket evinced no response. Did he disregard the message? Why did he not reply?

Did anyone know the portent of all this? But speculation was generally extinguished by anxious glances at the round face of the booking hall clock and a move to descend to the platform to view the signal with rising anticipation.

The home signal would fall in due course and eager eyes would scan the regions beyond the goods yard which could be glimpsed through the frame of the station 'tunnel' – a clutter of coal trucks mainly on the north side with the red, slatted wall of the forge's (hydraulic) press shop in the ultimate background. But the porter would now emerge from the dark recesses of the hoist.

In no time the exhaust of an approaching train would reverberate from the factory walls and through the station arch would emerge the longingly awaited front end profile of 9885 or one of her clan.

An empty carriage would be located and entered and soon we would be steaming under the Church Street bridge and towards Tayport and all her joys. Time now to glance around our carriage and recall these forgotten features. The twin racks, one now supporting our bulky case. Below them pictures of holiday venues to tempt the traveller. They always seemed to feature English resorts with promises of golden sands and low rainfall (specified in precise terms).

Coaching stock and line-side scenes

Hotels were advertised at these various seemingly divine resorts – railway hotels, all of them – and the passenger would be exhorted to write to the resident manager for the necessary tariff (what a strange word, I would think). Delectable spots such as Sheringham, Gorleston-on-sea or Clacton-on-sea would be advertised; or a stay recommended at Liverpool Street's Great Eastern Hotel (in London, no less!). Which wealthy persons could afford to travel so far and live in such splendour? – I would wonder. In retrospective contemplation, I wonder why there should have been all this obsession with the Great Eastern Sector? Did ex Great Eastern coaching stock provide the carriages of the 11.28 in these times – six years after the amalgamation?

By this time, Dysart would be passed and the familiar,

adjacent path would be unfolding on our left (dubbed the 'side of the line' and much traversed when walks were the order of the day). My aunt would quote from R.L. Stevenson:

> 'Faster than fairies, faster than witches,
> Bridges and houses, hedges and ditches,
> And charging along like troops in a battle,
> All through the meadows the horses and cattle.'

Soon we would be past Randolph Colliery and just beyond its spoil heaps (or bings, in colloquial parlance). At the foot of the embankment would be the wood, which seemed to be in the process of being swallowed up by an ever-growing pond, its trees seemingly stricken and in poor shape (but I knew nothing, then, of sulphur and its compounds nor of iron salts).

Then would come Thornton Junction, with all its bustle and diverging tracks. The massive pitfall had not yet commenced and

6. A typical south Fife scene in pre-war days. LNER Class J38 loco hauling coal wagons at approach to Dysart station at extremity of Loughborough Road. Note gas street lamp of ultimate design adopted by Kirkcaldy Town Council and privately owned wagons of Lochgelly Iron and Coal Co. (Photo: Author with Kodak No. 2 Brownie camera borrowed from aunt)

the station structures were still in their original red brick. I recall two tall buildings on the west side, gable-end to the track, gaunt in appearance and with pitched roofs. These must have been demolished early, and simultaneously with the erection of the many subsequent wooden structures which conveyed a concept of impermanence.

Positively recalled is the lofty viaduct before Markinch and the obligatory viewing of the Leven far below; and its derivative lade beside the Sythrum mills, whose tall unadorned chimney seemed almost as high as the viaduct itself.

The next point of positive recall is the long cutting, against whose massive retaining wall ran a ducted stream which was hard to discern between ballast and wall. On emerging from these subterranean regions we came to Falkland Road, where we stopped in these days, as we did at every other station *en route*.

On the ensuing descent was the mysterious tunnel to Kirkforthar limeworks (only finally identified and explained in 1943 with the publication of Mr George P. Bennet's excellent books on the industries and roads of that area). Immediately adjacent, the sweep of the Hangman's Brac and thc Cadger's Brae – as I now know these roads to be – excited my imagination as I contemplated to what far and unknown regions they might lead.

Ladybank was always a source of interest and I must have regarded it as being a very much larger railway centre than it was. Nevertheless it was a junction for Perth via Newburgh and Kinross via Auchtermuchty and Gateside (and ultimately Glasgow via Alloa and Stirling for those of sufficient patience and endurance). It possessed an engine shed, strategic dumps of locomotive coal and extensive civil engineering workshops.

At Hospital Mill Crossing I would wonder at the strange railway that seemed to run to the hills, on whose breast there stood these strange tower structures (in much later days identified as the Cults Lime Kilns). For long these exercised my curiosity and imagination, until a bicycle opened yet another dimension and the secret places revealed, at last, their wonders. Little did I contemplate the actuality of that curious realm of cavernous mines and earlier kilns, tucked away in seductive woodland neuks.

Further line-side scenes and shadows of an early accident

Springfield was also of interest, partly because of the large factory with its tall chimney set in a congested wooded valley below the station. What might it make? I pondered. Would it also have a large steam engine to provide power like those at home in Kirkcaldy?

Succeeding years disclosed its function: as a textile factory which was the successor to the handlooms of the village, as in not a few of Fife's villages. Beyond the opposite platform a road emerged from beneath the railway, obviously from that quarter, and from it diverged a rightward branch, while the main limb swept into the immediately adjacent village. To what exciting places would these roads lead?

Cupar came next – a place, seemingly, of towers and steeples, having a third line between the north- and south-bound tracks. (For what purpose I wondered?) Beyond the station through which it ran, there rose a large factory with many sidings and a signal box of its own. What was this – that involved such a density of traffic? I pondered. Had I but known, this was a recent arrival, which was to provide, in season, massive freight for the railway, from many a corner of Scotland and beyond, as trainload after trainload of sugarbeet was drawn to its copious reception sidings.

Then came Dairsie with its dimunitive station and goods yard, demanding another stop. Truly, after all these stops, we must be really far from home!

A winding river with a bridge and tree-lined slopes lay beyond. Somewhere in the background soared towering masts. What were these for? I queried. Something to do with wireless messages was the meaningless answer to my uncomprehending ear.

How interesting might it be, to explore such exciting regions – but so far away from home and known familiar territory! On the left, a road followed the lineside, like the one at Dysart, near home, but in this case from a pleasant farm with a most elaborate chimney. Did farms have boilers and engines? Surely not! Must find out about this enigma!

Into a deep cutting now, with heavy and impressive retaining walls and two bridges spanning it in quick succession. What a nice shady spot! I mused.

Now a glimpse of the road, which had crossed the second bridge and thereafter was winding away into the distance – and not a vehicle on it. Another intriguing call for exploration. To what enchanting spot might it lead?

Soon we were to cross a bridge with a stream beneath, winding through thick reed-beds to join another stream beyond, it seemed. Would that spot be marshy, down below? Might it be

7. The 'Swamp' lying eastwards of the main line. Taken from the Mill Aqueduct in the foreground. (Photo: Author c.1985)

unpleasant or even unsafe, perhaps? Definitely not a spot to venture into alone! Well, in the years after 1970 (forty-three years on!) I would find out – by walking through the 'swamp' on urgent business bound; but that I was not then to know.

Immediately beyond this confluence we steamed in to Leuchars Junction, where there were both north and south dock platforms and, to the east, a factory with three chimneys, one seeming exceeding tall.

Now we steamed straight ahead whilst the main line appeared to veer to the left round a green hill surmounted by an undefined little structure with a squat dome-like top. Hardly had we set off along this line than a curious little brick-built station slipped past with a signal box opposite in matching red brick, and a level crossing. How low these platforms seemed! The signalman was passing something to the driver (tablets and single line working were still to be discovered). On the right now stood a low red-brick structure, strangely decrepit (Leuchars gas works it now seems, though few of the locals seem to recall its presence).

The line ran straight for a time, now, with tall trees along the lineside, to reach a level crossing, with a cottage alongside. Then it went through a dense wood.

All of a sudden the line seemed to veer away to the left and as it veered, what a spectacle! A broad expanse of dark blue water dominated the right and on its far rim a real lighthouse – brilliantly white in the sunlight; near a glorious fringe of golden yellow sand and more of it on the near shore to which we seemed to close!

Still we curved; and the sea was narrowing now and the sandy dunes disappearing. Wood stacks in profusion, now, after another level-crossing and attendant signal box.

But the train had stopped at a signal. Gazing out of the left hand window, I could see a factory building with a curious open door on the first floor and boiler-suited men standing in the aperture studying the train. (Not a notion on my part, then, of Teagle Openings, far less of their regulation.) Between the railway and this factory (later identified as the sawmill) ran a road, with its pavement abutting a low stone boundary wall to the line on which we paused.

A shriek from the engine whistle and we were moving once again, as we crawled slowly into Tayport, past the outer home signal now in the clear position. Yearly, I would witness the repetition of this manoeuvre, but it would be many years before I discovered that the procedure had resulted from a sad accident in November 1881 when a 21-wagon coal train from Ladybank had been run into by a passenger train, causing loss of life. The poor signalman at Tayport, who had daily worked incredible hours (6.20 a.m. till 10.06 p.m.), was charged in the court but given a not guilty verdict. Thereafter, it was decreed that all north-bound trains should be brought to a stand at the outer home signal before being allowed to proceed. Our train, of course, crossed the up Edinburgh train at Tayport but the latter was by that time over the points and stationary at the up platform.

My journey, which would be repeated many times, was at an end.

The time had come to prepare the luggage and lower the window, as the canopied station exit came slowly into view.

Harbours old and new; 'puffers'; dredging; bobbins

Slowly the train drew into the north platform of Tayport station and stopped towards the extremity of the platform. There we alighted, to join my uncle in walking up to the house by Dalgleish Street and Commonty Road. This route ran parallel to the railway; and at a point closer to our destination provided a wide sweep of the river and a view, which included not only at least two thirds of Dundee but also that portion of the Angus coast between that city and Monifeith.

This vista also encompassed the branch-line rising steadily to the horizon. The impact of this view seldom ceased to impress; and it was only with the total disappearance of the railway and a resulting, fundamental change in the vegetation of the West Common that some of the magic departed.

Till the departure of the railway and the consequent cataclysmic changes to the harbour and its environs (which till then was a railway facility) the station and harbour drew me to them as a magnet.

What a hive of activity was that region! At various times esparto and timber boats were discharged and trawlers were coaled. In summer the Railway Company's bucket-dredger *Almond* would dredge the harbour. In the earliest years, the mussel-dredgers would still operate some of their 'Puffers', and these subsequently continued supine at their moorings for many a day. In the adjacent lyes wagons would be marshalled. Timber wagons would be unloaded in the sawmill yards and horse-drawn loads of timber continued to be moved betwixt the sawmill and its encircling yards. Regularly, material would be moved to the iron foundry.

Adjacent to the old harbour was a quaint, diminutive wood-turning or bobbin-mill with a small steam drive, including a

8. Rail approach to Tayport from the south. Station and signal box in background; water tower and engine shed on left; coal/freight sidings to right. (Photo: Author, late 1940s)

diminutive external condenser and slender steel smoke-stack. Small boats would come and go. In that quarter a ramp rose from the water of the old harbour to a brick structure of antique appearance. It had brick underworks and a tarred wooden superstructure (on which I recall seeing the carcass of a sea-creature – possibly a seal – on one early holiday visit).

Meantime, at the station, adjacent, there would be the daily procession of trains to both north and south. Even today, some thirty-five or so years on, it is hard to believe that all has gone – but what a lure it then was for one with a railway interest!

CHAPTER 3

Running round; coupling and uncoupling; a night scene

All the local Dundee to Tayport trains had to have the engine moved to the reverse end of the train for the return journey and this 'run-round' operation was a never-failing source of interest and, indeed, a mandatory experience if one arrived for a Dundee train well ahead of its departure time. The duties of the fireman down between engine and coaches while the driver set back or took up the strain on the coupling was guaranteed to send a shiver down the spine and induced a question of how one would react if designated this duty. Thus it seemed as if, subconsciously perhaps, one was setting up an unstated series of manhood targets (or perhaps virility checks):

Crossing unknown swamps;
Exploring far-away roads to unknown destinations;
Coupling up locomotives;
Operating machinery;
Firing boilers;
Travelling to London;
Writing for a tariff at some high-class hotel;
Travelling to some of the 'exotic' resorts depicted in those carriage-pictures of yore.

All such unspecified challenges lurked, it would seem, in the subconscious. As one grew up, or extended one's experience and in a manner that approximated to the attainment of these self-defined 'unachievable' objectives of early childhood (acknowledge it or not), there was a sense of having advanced into a higher sphere of existence implied by such achievements.

One came to realise with amazement that in principle at least – excluding any evaluation of the quality or intensity of their execution – one had conquered them all. At the end of a tortuous trail, involving much sweat and no small burning of the midnight candle, yet with nothing to record in the world's accepted terms, perhaps these mundane achievements are all that can be asked from life (other than ethical achievements, if any minuscule count can be made in that department, possibly the only one of any true significance).

The run-round operation seemed even more daunting in the winter evenings, and in the passage of years it would be witnessed at various New Year holiday seasons or on other brief, parental forays (for sundry family reasons).

One such impression from a very early visit lingers in the memory. How strident are such otherwise fragmentary snatches! The journey to the station, seated on my father's shoulders, on a winter's evening when the heavy frost made his every footstep ring and each breath became instantaneously visible in the lamp-lit night.

We turned down the lane into Commonty Road and, on a sudden, before us appeared all the fascinating splendour of a night-time Angus coastline – an unending series of twinkling lights, whose foremost were reflected in the murky waters of the Tay and rose in tier after tier, all the way from Dundee City to Broughty Castle and well beyond. The lighthouses at Buddon and the Pile sent their shafts of light across the waters; and here and there shone the tiny reds and greens of unspecified navigation markers from ship or pier.

There was the usual heightened excitement of the night: of the locality in its unfamiliar, magical garb; the fear of a missed train. Down Dalgleish Street we went between venerable dwellings: the domiciles of seamen, mussel-dredgers, whalers and ferrymen from days of old.

Suddenly on the night air came the deep rumble of an approaching train entering its rocky cut. The regulator was shut and drifting down, no doubt with tablet at the ready for the signal man stationed ready, below his box beside the foot-bridge. But our steps quickened then as in through the tunnel-like station doorway we hastened to witness yet another ritual of un-coupling and re-coupling as the Westinghouse pump drummed its familiar tune.

Chapter 4

'Auld Reekie' and a Scott on the Sleeper

I recall another evening experience of several years later (c.1932, I now estimate). This relates to a summer evening occurrence at Dundee's Tay Bridge station whither my aunt had brought me in a change of trains, after a visit to Arbroath, where my mother and brother had been on holiday.

As we awaited the arrival of the Tayport local train, the London sleeper drew in to the southbound through platform – double-headed by the NBR Atlantic 'Auld Reekie' and a four-coupled engine which I now believe to have been of the Scott class (though it just might have been an earlier four-coupled engine). This was my first and only positive recollection of an NBR Atlantic. I was duly impressed by the bulk of the locomotive and by the twin engine combination. It was, indeed, a night to be remembered. The mere fact of being up so late, and in such a busy spot at that hour, was sufficient in itself to warrant recall.

I was intrigued by the sleeping compartments, which appealed to my imagination. Those which I recall must have been of the old 'four-in-a-compartment' units, as I recall the top berths and their tartan rugs (which in later years I would often sample on the West Coast line out of Glasgow Central on journeys to Euston, Birmingham and the English Midlands). The facets of that evening remain strong: the surge of passengers; the glow from the footplate; the echoes of multiple exhausts in that sunken place.

Subsequently we departed from the dock at the south end beside the buffers of which stood the inevitable (Pintsch-Oil?)

9. 'High Girders' viewed from rear of diesel multiple unit train ex Tayport for Dundee. (Photo: E. Macleod)

10. NBR Atlantics at Hawick shed on 'the Waverley Road' in 1910. (From the collection of the late Mr R.B. Haddon and presented to the author by Mr Haddon.)

gas-tanker wagon, with that curious inscription: 'NOT TO BE TAKEN THROUGH SHILDON TUNNEL'. Why not? I would subsequently wonder, on many a further occasion. What dire consequences would follow disregard of this warning? At that time I had not studied loading gauges for coaching and general stock nor plotted out the phenomenon of vehicle overthrow on curves; nor had I investigated the related problems of buffer-lock, the first of which conditions, I eventually concluded, might be one basis for this peremptory command.

Our ultimate departure was also of interest, with a slow, climbing glimpse of the LNER shed on the right with its numerous locomotives and the illuminated windows of its lean-to offices, with figures glimpsed, moving around in silhouette, and its whole environs in a state of bustle at what (for me) was a late hour.

But this scrutiny was limited for we were now steaming up the bridge approach through Esplanade station and rounding the entering curve over the unseen inverted bow-string spans to gain the bridge proper, soon to enter W.H. Barlow's reconstruction of the 'High Girders'. Eyes were now focused to the left for a sighting of those ill-fated stumps round which still swirled the dark waters. The eyes were drawn down the river, however, by the never-failing attraction of these riverside lights, which made an enchanting fairyland of both sides of the estuary.

The vision was soon usurped by the hypnotic rhythm created by the shadows from the diagonal girder-bracings as they danced across the carriage floor in continuing procession, inducing thoughts of that final swing in 1879, of which I had been told and which still produced fleeting but dark imaginings.

Now they were gone! and there was the signal box and the retreating figure of its occupant bearing back to the lighted regions of its interior after delivery of the inevitable single-line tablet.

A stop now at Wormit. (Did some giant specimen live there in days of old to lend it such a name? I wondered.)

11. Scene westwards of Illustration 1, grade still rising. West Lighthouse and Dundee's Law Hill will be noted. (Valentine postcard, postmark 29 November 1927)

A continuous screech now, as wheel flange ground on rail and we snaked through the tight tunnel curves and emerged at the rear of tidy villas where lit windows betokened approaching normality and ultimate banishment to bed and an end to all these fascinating events.

On now, through the Newports (West then East), with the dark and gloomy night-mysteries of girder-spanned Berry's Den between; to seek the summit by the gas works and to make that glorious, effortless descent and experience the first-time opportunity to witness Tayport's West Light in full beam.

Chapter 5

Pre-war Dundee: its docks, sandboats and teeming streets

Railways featured strongly in the dockside scene at Dundee and so the city was for me yet another fascination of childhood days. As I grew older a visit to Dundee with my aunts became a regular feature of the summer sojourn in Tayport. Occasionally the journey to the city would be by train, but as my aunt found the long exit steps at Tay Bridge Station and the uphill return by Dalgleish Street somewhat formidable, the bus and ferry mode was much favoured. This was not my preferred route, but who was I to decide such issues? In any case, the ferry journey had the delectable compensation of allowing one to watch the operation of the vessel's diagonal steam engines, as well as viewing the river and its shipping from another new and exciting angle. In addition, our route took us up past the LNER and LMS passenger and goods stations, from the latter of which emerged rail-lines set in to the causeway sets, which crossed the roadway to gain access to the network of extensive dock-sidings.

There was always the possibility, too, that one of the small four-coupled, dock shunting engines might be seen. These were absolutely different from all other engines in my ken. They were, in fact, LNER class Y9 engines and each pulled behind it its little wooden service truck containing its coal supply. The cabs were rudimentary, open affairs and the chimneys were crowned with a roughly hemispheric spark arrester, which somehow imparted a primal backwoods-ish air to the whole scene. They were preceded by a shunter with a red flag, who had red markings on his uniform – as I imperfectly recall – the red elements of flag and garb being dingy in appearance, as of great age and usage.

To the right of the road from the Craig Pier was located a

murky chasm in which was situated the main line to Aberdeen, at the point of entry into the serpentine mysteries of Dock Street Tunnel, and from which soared the signal post for Dundee East Box, down below at the station extremity. Ne'er a glimpse of a locomotive could be seen there, the nearest to any evidence of their presence being, perhaps, a violent blast of smoke and steam coupled to ominous subterranean rumbles, after the clatter of the 'boards' dropping to their off position.

One of the dockside connections, having crossed from the old LNE goods station, passed through a sparred wooden gate and ran between the stone-parapet-crowned protective brick wall, which defined the main-line cutting, and a totally begrimed gable wall of a multi-storey tenement building. Seldom if ever did we encounter traffic on this line.

As one crossed to Union Street, a smart glance to the right took in that part of the harbour much frequented by sand boats, survivors from another life, which dredged the sand from the multitudinous banks in the estuary and discharged their take into rail wagons positioned along the quayside.

Great numbers of heavily-laden carts were horse-drawn to and from station yards and the harbour region. Not a few carried the Wordie logo, they being the accredited carters for the LMS, whose extensive goods station lay between the Taybridge passenger station of the LNER and the elaborately-fronted passenger station of the successors to the 'Caley' (Dundee West).

All was bustle and stir.

To me, Dundee, at that early juncture in life, was the archetypal city, seething with life, a teeming mass of activity and humanity. Possibly this was because its still-overcrowded slums were intermixed, or at least cheek by jowl, with shopping and commercial enclaves as well as industrial plants; their inhabitants intermingled with their fellow citizens: working, shopping, sightseeing or generally going about whatever business they had in hand. There was a vibrancy in the air, a sense of life, however raw and to a degree remote from that of my sheltered existence to date.

Chapter 6

Fettykill – 1930s experience of a closed branch

South Fife itself produced its own railway experiences of unique and pleasurable recall. Each summer in June there was a Sunday School trip. The destination provided, faithfully followed a standard rotation along the line to the north, seemingly moving steadily northward as year followed year before retracing the sequence. One started at Markinch and progressed through Kingskettle to Ladybank and thence back to Markinch.

In one very early year, before I became aware of the formula (1933, I suspect), the trip went to Leslie, the terminus of a branch from Markinch, which opened in 1861 and closed to passenger traffic on 4th January 1932. This line (which itself had a freight branch to serve the Rothes and Auchmuty paper mills and a siding for Balbirnie paper mill) crossed the river Leven twice on tall, impressive stone viaducts. The second was located just before the terminus. At the end of this viaduct, yet another branch went off to Fettykil paper mills, and this mill in particular kept the branch alive as all coal to the mills came along the branch. In the early days the branch had, no doubt, brought in esparto or wood-pulp, chlorine, clay and miscellaneous requirements to the Auchmuty and Rothes Mills if not to all of them. Material was supplied by rail to some of them till the 1950s at least and certain items till as late as the nineties. In the early days finished paper in vans was railed to Markinch for the journey south.

An excellent record of the bridge remains in photographic form. A director of the adjacent Fettykil mill, the late W.J.V.

Anderson, was a superb railway photographer and has recorded the viaduct and its railway environs amongst a supreme album of railway scenes from the 'Kingdom'.

The trip to Leslie seemed to have additional 'unknown' and mysterious ingredients included. Even then, the passenger service had been withdrawn so the tracks seemed unusually grassy while I recall rabbits scurrying about the track in droves.

On these trips there was much flying of paper streamers from the carriages and rigidly enforced adult instructions to keep away from windows seemed to be less stringent for the event. Thus, unusual views were obtained. To this day I recall gazing backward along the track as the Leslie viaduct receded into the distance and woods appeared on one side of the track.

Only once did I return, some thirty-seven years later on a special excursion to explore some of Fife's closed branches. Now all the woods and fields have vanished and the last viaduct and part of the track bed provide a pedestrian way. The immense new town of Glenrothes now covers the area and it would be nigh impossible to identify the old landmarks.

There was, of course, the joy of watching the engine run round its train at Markinch before we steamed southward by busy Thornton junction with all its shunting activities and a complex of branching tracks to the East Neuk, Methil and Dunfermline. Then came the climb to the summit near Randolph Pit and down through Dysart to Sinclairtown, our point for detraining.

These were busy times for the railways with multiple reserved accommodation on scheduled trains and special trains into the bargain, all filled with happy and streamer-flying groups. These hectic scenes are vividly recalled; as is the pervading ebullient spirit. It must be nigh impossible for any visitor viewing today's railways to recapture or, in any authentic way, to visualise the railway scene in these happy days of childhood.

Chapter 7

By train through South Fife; A whistle from 'Ole Bill'; sundry local excursions; shunted up the bank; the Forth bridge and anticipating the Fife circle

Other trips there were, however.

Through the agency of our primary school teacher (a most excellent and effective teacher) many of the class attended the Scripture Union activities; and, by universal acclaim, it was agreed that their parties and trips were in a 'super' bracket, being much more lavish than anything the Sunday School could provide. Their trips went to much more exciting destinations and as we were not accompanied by our parents we seemed to have a much greater element of freedom (albeit they were very responsibly run).

Thus one year we went to a Dunfermline park situated hard by the railway, from which some of the boys, myself included, explored Dunfermline Glen and had an excellent day, which was never to be forgotten. In another year we went by the East-Fife Coastal Railway to Elie and had another glorious day amidst the sands and dunes of its delectable coastline. Ladybank saw yet another highly successful excursion. All of these were by train and extended intimately a knowledge of the Fife network.

At Sunday School, a few years earlier, the talk after lessons got round to an exhibition that was advertised for that weekend and was voted, by general class acclaim, an absolute 'must'. It had been organised by the LNER in the Kirkcaldy Goods Yard to demonstrate railway facilities, and at that venue there were gathered examples of the latest coaches and wagons, together with a steam breakdown crane and a variety of locomotives in steam.

The footplate of one was made accessible to the public and by contributing some minor sum to the local cottage hospital fund, one was allowed to blow the whistle. There were no qualms about noise pollution in those days, in a town with a battery of steam hammers and a thrice-daily chorus of factory sirens and the crescendo of Nairn's fire siren on Saturday at noon, which was, by definition, of a glorious stridency. This engine was NBR, J36 class: 'Ole Bill' (9661) which had seen active service in Flanders during the Great War.

This exhibition, I reckoned exhilarating in the extreme; and during the course of our scrutinies, my father was able to draw my attention to many a technical feature that I might otherwise have missed.

The railways were used for travel as a matter of course in those days, although the as yet unamalgamated bus companies were making steady inroads into the passenger market and by 1932 or so had eliminated the old Wemyss Tramway's 'Mustard Boxes' and were to oust the Kirkcaldy tram cars completely by 1931. If, therefore, there was an odd trip to Aberdour Sands on a Saturday afternoon, it was by train that we went; and we returned in the same manner.

One return is recalled because of the train passing operation at Kirkcaldy, where it was a matter of 'everyone out' of the 'slow', while it was shunted up the bank or siding in the cutting ahead to allow the following express through. On its departure, back again our train shunted (empty per the rule book) and in we all poured for the single-station journey to the next station down the line – Sinclairtown.

Likewise, when my aunt and her friend took me with them on a day trip to Dunfermline and its Pittencrieff Glen, it was again by train that we travelled, going via Thornton on the outward journey and returning via Inverkeithing, traversing a portion of the circuit executed by today's 'Fife Circle' trains, which now of course, utilise the former freight and mineral spur at Thornton South. In these early days this was all new territory to me and we passed many collieries where the non-condensing winding-engines blasted into the atmosphere great billowing plumes. I have often pondered on the exact location of these and, in certain instances, have conjectured correctly; but these distant forays into unknown lands have left no positive identification in the memory.

If there was a rare excursion to Edinburgh (with its zoo and castle), again the mode of transport was the train and this allowed a crossing of the mighty Forth Bridge. This was seen to even greater advantage a few years later when a Saturday afternoon excursion was made to Dalmeny (where a walk to Cramond was planned). This safari enabled us to walk under these massive girders, illustrated dramatically in that treasured railway book by Cecil J. Allen – possession of which, perhaps, had been a powerful stimulus for this prevailing interest in railway matters.

Chapter 8

Meccano Magazine as a source of railway knowledge; observations in South Fife; coal engines 0-6-0; 0-6-2 and others

Probably the most popular toy devised for boys has been the Meccano set, of which many of my contemporaries were fortunate possessors, in widely varying degrees of sophistication. Their associated product, the Hornby train, was equally popular and was much desired by many of my chums. These products could be quite elaborate and extensive and the price would correspond. I was fortunate in having modest units of both types and derived great pleasure from them.

Meccano, of course, produced the famous and eponymous magazine, which not only gave instruction and advice on both products but dealt with a very wide range of topics including engineering and railway issues, which extended my interest in such matters. When I could, I read this journal avidly. Though I was not fortunate enough to be a regular subscriber to the journal, I was indeed fortunate in being given odd sums of money by friends of the family and relatives and such sums would be judiciously channelled in this direction. Looking back on these times, I now realise how much pleasure I derived from that source.

It certainly stimulated a lively interest in the railway scene and provided a basic knowledge of, and literacy in, that subject. I only now realise fully that it was to extend my geographical horizons and inspire a desire to visit some of the frequently described locations where locomotives performed or were built or shedded. Even today there is a quickening of the pulse if one of these points is visited or stumbled upon, even though the initial source of the interest has vanished or has become little more than an industrial estate or yet another featureless housing development.

Slowly the picture of locomotive operation grew and the function of the locomotive shed became apparent. There was a stimulus to learn more of the locomotive and an increasing desire to watch these fascinating machines whenever possible.

Fortunately line-side observation was a relatively easy matter in South Fife, lying as it did in proximity to rich sectors of the coalfield and having two major coal-exporting docks close at hand. Movement of coal was a salient local function of the railway system and so engendered much locomotive operation in collieries, yards and sidings as well as on main lines. Many of the locomotives involved were of NBR design and though it would be some time before specific identification could be made and a greater time till their basic design differences could be assimilated and fully understood, recognition was growing and J35, 36 and 37 classes were soon identifiable.

A key point for such activities lay around Dysart station, slightly to the north of which branched off the line to Frances Colliery or the Dubby as it was universally known locally. Trains were made up and despatched from a small yard adjacent to the junction and a superbly situated line-side path (referred to earlier) gave an excellent vantage point for all this activity. The pit branch crossed the adjacent main road by a level crossing and from there a footpath was separated from it only by a wire-and-stob fence, from which close-up viewing could be practised. There could be much sound and fury as well as pyrotechnic displays implied in the adjacent passage of an NBR 'S' or LNER J37 and a close up of side rod motion at close quarters.

Elsewhere, the local harbour was shunted daily by a J88 class locomotive, which could be viewed at very close quarters. The rail approach to the harbour was down the very steep Harbour Branch, which was easily observed from certain strategically sited over- as well as under-bridges and, like the main line, from certain ideally and contiguously sited main and side streets.

Shunting was a continuous operation at both Sinclairtown and Kirkcaldy, in those cases by six-coupled 'shunters' of Great Eastern origin which in part were visible from adjacent roadways. Six-coupled engines therefore featured prominently in my early attempts to keep some note of the engines seen. Even at this late juncture, numbers such as 9117, 9192 and 6883 lurk in the memory.

A few years would elapse till treks on foot (with little restriction on sensible access) would allow close viewing of the Methil branch through 'the Wemyss Firs' or the former little yards near Thornton South, where the latter would display an N15 on marshalling duties.

And so the knowledge grew and, simultaneously, an insatiable desire to see more!

Chapter 9

Transformers by rail and road-engine; emergence of the square deal era; a D1 in rural Fife; the advent of the A4 Class

From across the years, how many and how varied are the railway vignettes that can be drawn from the well of memory and from every ascending level of experience. The majority are mere passing incidents, though encapsulating cheerful, stirring and evocative scenes. Others are of a less strident hue, being more of the khaki or dun of the daily round, but stubbornly retained as part of the erstwhile commonplace that has gone forever but is now of pleasurable recall.

One such relates to one of a host of holiday weekends spent in Newburgh-on-Tay. My maternal grandfather, who seemed to have an infallible ear for all such events, advised that the next Monday morning was the scheduled time for the movement of a large (by contemporary standards) transformer to the new switching and transforming station at Ferryfield. My notion of date is now vague; but I should imagine that it would have been in the mid 1930s. The transformer was to arrive by rail at Newburgh goods yard and was to be drawn by traction engine from the point of unloading to the sub-station just to the east of Abernethy, near Ferryfield.

Grandfather, Father and myself arrived at the juncture when the transformer had just been loaded on to its road gondola and the two steam traction engines were being coupled on for the mile or so journey over the nearby Fife border. That was a brave sight, as I recall it, with the road engines immaculately polished and a feather at their safety valves as they prepared for the big starting pull.

We followed down on to the main road, I highly reluctant to relinquish such a unique and pleasing spectacle. Somehow, later, when I bought a new mill transformer and saw it enter the mill, there was a submerged sensation of having achieved some unarticulated desire to emulate that scene of possibly three decades before. Incidentally, though the dates and sequences of events have perished, I recall that the three of us later went to the day of opening and public access. There, I gazed with totally uncomprehending eyes on transformers, switch-gear and capacitors, though the shining insulators, mighty pylons and general aura of potential hazard left a powerful impression.

Just as this Newburgh episode presaged the swing from steam prime movers, so the threat to the supremacy of rail as an unquestioned mover of men and materials was borne in to me in that same spot. On a later weekend, my grandfather announced that the double track beyond Newburgh was to be singled to save costs. No doubt this was around the start of the 'Square Deal for Rail' campaign, which only terminated with the advent of war and governmental control (events which the privatisation exponents will possibly and fervently hope to forget).

As I recall, double track was to be retained between Glenburnie Junction and a location around Cluniefield Bridge. Certainly, as the years advanced, passenger traffic from Ladybank diminished to a degree. The war probably saw a certain injection of both passenger and freight traffic (possibly to avoid the gruelling climb through Glenfarg), and continued at reasonable levels till the national pattern of robust road-haulage ingress in the post-war years. But the railway had its advantages until effective-subsidisation of road building on a massive scale eliminated the remnants.

Such consideration recalls another Newburgh week-end incident related to a period of very heavy snowfall. By Monday the bus services had totally capitulated. My parents and I (like many more bound for Kirkcaldy and beyond) had, perforce, to travel home by train and it was 'as of old' to see the Ladybank train packed. My lasting impression of that occasion is of standing in a crowded corridor watching the snow-covered hills around Lindores Loch sweep past.

A much later recollection is of a snowy winter's day in 1944 in Glenburnie, *en route* by bicycle to Kirkcaldy. The compelling blast of an engine had echoed from Clatchard Crag, and I paused to observe the nature of the locomotive and its train. As I watched, the signal for the Ladybank line came off and I set off at a good pace through Lindores village to achieve a suitable vantage point by the lochside. A mixed freight drew in to view, with a 4-4-0 at its head, making good headway. No NBR 'four-coupled' this, however, but an engine whose Ramsbottom type safety valves and tender fittings (amongst other characteristics) marked it as of (English) GNR parentage. Enthusiastically, I followed its passage and my last view was of its entry in to Collesie Den as I counted its load from the bridge near the end of the loch.

Some passing scenes leave a disproportionate impression to their duration, if the subject observed is of prime interest. Thus it was at my first viewing of Gresley's streamlined A4 class of locomotives. Well I remember the day in 1937 when this was achieved. Two classmates and I were on a ramble, with a mentor who was some years older, along the rocky shore between Kirkcaldy and Kinghorn. Our companion, an enthusiastic locomotive photographer, suddenly announced that he believed that a new class of locomotive was being introduced on the Aberdeen to Edinburgh Expresses and that these were to be introduced, initially, on Saturday timetables.

It was mutually agreed that we should climb up on to the high point of the most adjacent embankment to view events, as he believed the afternoon train was imminent. The timing was masterly, for he had just time to set up his camera when up the line came my first A4.

That moment in time is encapsulated for today's viewing (with three classmates as part of the scene). A print of the

12. LNER A4 Class Pacific, on one of its earliest Saturday turns of duty between Aberdeen and Edinburgh. Taken near Kinghorn. (Photo: Mr C. Godden, 1937)

photograph was given to me and after some vicissitudes, when it was presumed lost, it remains in my possession.

It was many a year afterwards before I was able to photograph engines myself (as I devoutly wished to do) – and then it was with a borrowed camera. When I eventually acquired a camera of my own, commensurate with the desired product quality and – more crucially perhaps – found the essential time to use it, steam locomotion was largely of the past. Such is life, however, and such disappointments must be low down on the scale of essentials, though the lost opportunities for catching such golden moments still rankle.

CHAPTER 10

The 'Cock o' the North'

One salient locomotive memory relating to the summer of 1934 stands out. At that time there was excited talk, even amongst those who were by no means locomotive aficionados, of a strange new engine running on the old NBR main line through Fife. My assimilation of locomotive engineering knowledge was still in a primitive stage and so a technically accurate and detailed assessment of the features which indicated the advances of the new design could only be discussed in a simple and stilted manner. Even a cursory, initial glance at the newcomer, none-the-less, indicated that it was vastly different from the fundamental lineaments of its older and more conservative brethren of NBR parentage or even from the more recent sophisticates from the master hand of H.N. Gresley.

My father, whose place of work lay directly adjacent to the main line, was the first of my circle to see this new wonder. Though not one who studied locomotives in a detailed manner, but as one whose work had been centred on them at an early point in his career, he had a keen appreciation of the species and loved to watch and admire as an express locomotive would thunder through at the head of a heavy express to Aberdeen or other mainline destination. He duly related the details of his sighting and in the process whetted my appetite intensely.

But tales were also circulated at school and, very soon, in that forum for discussion of all things new or wonderful, the Sunday School class, in the post-lesson period, there were whispers of greater size, greater tractive effort and modern design features. Whether I comprehended the implications of the rotary cam-operated poppet-valve gear or the full objectives of the ACFI feed-water heater, I very much doubt. Much mention was made of the locomotive in the papers at that time and every scrap I, no doubt, read avidly.

Though failing detail-memory forbids me to record the siting categorically, my father referred to seeing her go by with the engineer's wooden indicator-card shelter mounted between smokebox-front and buffer-beam. I feel fairly certain of this, however, as I recall demanding, consequently, an explanation of indicator cards: their constitution, production and analysis, though in an informal manner.

Shortly after these interchanges and sightings the holiday period came round and I learned that our destination was to be Tayport, which could include a journey to Dundee. I could scarcely wait for the departure, which might just bring a sighting of the new engine.

To my joy, while awaiting the local connection at Dundee–Tay Bridge Station, there reverberated the exhaust of a mighty locomotive and the strident hiss of opened cylinder drains, as in from the south rushed an express – drawn by none other than the Cock o' the North. Without regard to the feelings of startled fellow-travellers, or, indeed, for any other such mundane considerations, I rushed in a triumphant dash along the length of the lengthy platform until I apparently came to its utmost end. But still the locomotive was beyond my reach, for the newcomer itself lay beyond the normal extremity of the platform – or that portion of it that was permitted to passengers – in a chasm-like region, much begrimed and symptomatic of Dundee's manufacturing grime though generated by the railway smoke of years.

Hope there was still, however. A narrow strip of platform extended for several feet beyond this point, to terminate in a steep ramp. Along this precarious ledge I ran, and here, amidst a small band of like-minded enthusiasts, I stood in astonishment and wonder and viewed the gleaming symmetry of the monster. There I was rooted, gazing in admiration and awe at the polished

13. Loco 'Lord President'. Same class as 'Cock o' the North'. After its rebuilding with Walschaert's motion and exhaust injector. (Tractive effort: 41,440 lb.) (Valentine postcard bought 1939)

green locomotive before me, as steam now rushed from its squat safety-valves with a deafening hiss.

Here indeed was a creation of wonder, besides which the Scotts, the Glens, the Directors and even, perhaps, the impressive Pacifics were dwarfed into lesser significance.

The enthusiasm was not entirely misplaced, for at the time of the inaugural runs she was the most powerful engine of her day and O.S. Nock in his *Locomotives of Sir Nigel Gresley* records a drawbar-horsepower during a journey to London of 2090 h.p. and a speed during trials of 85 m.p.h.

Chapter 11

A zone ticket and a memorable evening excursion

One summer holiday (possibly in 1935), it was decided that as my maternal grandparents were having a week of holiday coincident with the Kirkcaldy Trades Week, we should stay in their house and use Newburgh as a holiday base. My father had noticed that the LNER were issuing 'zone tickets'; and so he purchased a ticket for a zone based on or including the Newburgh area. This I considered an excellent proposition (and so, I believe, it worked out in actuality).

That ticket was certainly well used and many and varied were the journeys made. The longest journey, however, involved purchase of an additional ticket from Dundee as we travelled to Aberdeen to a region far beyond my ken (into what I believed to be, indeed, 'a far country'). I was naturally much excited, both in anticipation and in execution. To me the Aberdeen expresses were entirely in a superior category to my usual trains: not only in speed and distance-travelled but in the nature of the engines rostered and in overall prestige.

The journey also included, of necessity, a traversal of the 'North of Fife Line' and the Tay Bridge, as well as a change of trains at Tay Bridge Station which invariably had great potential for locomotive viewing and for scrutiny of all aspects of railway operation. There was also the journey along the Tay fringe at Broughty Ferry, where my familiar and adored happy hunting grounds at Tayport could be viewed – though at a distance – as an inversion of the familiar yearly process.

Arbroath and Montrose were noted with interest and not long after the latter came the 'hallowed' railway ground of Kinnaber

Junction (though its significance was diminished in these comparatively early days of railway awareness). For some unaccountable reason, a mental picture of Carmont signalbox lingers in the mind, probably for its stark Caley profile, which was unusual – for one from without 'Caley' territory. Seeing it fly past some years later, on a 1955 journey, I knew my location exactly on that unaccustomed main-line.

A memorable day was passed, seeing the sights of that northern city, including the great crater of Rubislaw granite-quarry with its Blondin crane to take in supplies and extract materials.

At departure came all the excitements of the 'joint' station with a glimpse of the London sleepers marshalled therein, and the Gresley engines that were to draw them south. No less exciting was the swift journey south, especially the spirited dash from Arbroath to Dundee, with the Tay estuary and all its familiar landmarks flashing past at a great speed, only to subside to a crawl through Dock Street tunnel with flange on rail playing a banshee tune through these tight curves within its melancholy and moist domain.

Sorry I was when we had to leave the train at Cupar and seek much more mundane transport home.

Yet, incredibly, an equally memorable journey was to come towards midweek. Strolling through the town, a poster was espied, proclaiming an evening excursion to a number of towns including St Andrews. Such excursions were commonplace for the LNER in those days and the relevant poster is well-remembered for its evocative portrayal of a dark and starry evening sky merging into gradations of lighter, early-evening shades. This was agreed upon as a highly desirable exercise and at the prescribed time we all arrived at the station: my parents, myself and brother as well as my cousin, aunt and uncle.

It transpired that two trains were planned to cover the advertised destinations. Eagerly, as ever, I scanned the tracks to the west and saw an approaching train edge through Cluniefield

Bridge and steam towards us. A 'double header'? Could it really be so? This might be fun! What a strange combination, I thought, as it edged up the platform. A 'Shire' and a 4-4-2 (C15) Tank. But the train formation was split and the 'Shire' took the lion's share of the coaches, leaving the 'Tankie' with a very modest train.

Off steamed the 'Shire' leaving our St Andrews 'special' champing at the bit. Soon, however, with but a minor delay, we also were off.

The mellow light of an early summer's evening made that incomparable river panorama even more astonishingly beautiful, viewed from that shelf at old Clatchard's base as we steamed forth. That vast mass, inconceivably, was to be blasted to nought across the years and now, the magnificent prehistoric fort, Wallace's Seat/Well and all, has vanished from human sight. Below rose the Mare's Craig, also scheduled to be quarried away, with old Denmylne of the Balfours close at hand.

But Glenburnie had been reached and with tablet on board – North of Fife – here we come!

Some such wild notion must have entered the driver's head, or he was behind a time which only he knew or – to be uncharitable – he had some personal reason for reaching St Andrews at the earliest hour. At any rate, no sooner had he passed Lindores than he set off at the most incredible speed so that the carriage lurched and swung and it was literally almost impossible to stay on the seats and to avoid being thrown on to the floor. Many times I have looked back to that journey to test my memories of it, so unlikely did these recollections seem. My parents, however, had identical recollections so it is not the offshoot of some mental aberration.

At that stage of existence I had no method of checking the speed nor, indeed, a watch. Never had St Fort arrived so rapidly. There on the main line the driver had to utilise the crossover to run round his train after yielding up the tablet and, duly coupled on to the reverse end of the train, we steamed more sedately back to Leuchars South Junction where we picked up yet another tablet for the St Andrews Branch and curved eastwards off the main line.

There, I noted to my amazement that the embankment embraced the 'swamp' so often noted on journeys north to Tayport, and the bridge entered therefrom lay almost above the confluence of the waters (in years much later, defined as the Motray Water and the Moonzie Burn).

The factory with the three chimneys was the next 'weel kent' landmark to loom in sight. In a short time we were steaming very close to it with only the width of a deserted roadway between. Through Guardbridge station – for such it was, with a signalbox and level crossing followed by a curving bridge above a wide river – and thence alongside dunes beside another estuary and

14. The 'Swamp' from the east with piers of former bridge that carried the St Andrews branch. Mill aqueduct in background. This is the point of confluence of the Motray Water coming under a bridge carrying the line to the north with the Moonzie Burn flowing parallel to the railway after passing under the line slightly further south through a heavily reinforced bridge beloved of a succession of local 'Tarzans' as the 'Beamie Brig'. (Photo: Author, c.1985)

15. English Electric Battery Electric Loco, within Guardbridge paper mill ('Grass Boiler'–Digester–pend). This had its official acceptance test in May 1925. Built at Dick Korr works, Preston. (Tractive effort 4,200 lb.) (Author's collection given by the late Mr James Brown. Possibly mid 1930s)

swinging round: Lo! the towers and ruins of St Andrews in whose sunken station we soon detrained.

After a pleasant evening spent in the mellow joys of a St Andrews that had not been ravaged by the motor car, the time for return came. The return journey was in total contradistinction to the wild abandoned flight of our outward journey. It was a most tranquil and pleasant evening with the valley of North Fife appearing lush and mellow as ever.

After reversal at St Fort we steamed sedately through the pastoral evening calm of Kilmany and by the quaint rustic siding beyond Rathillet and so to the multi-piered skew over-bridge at Parbroath, there to enter the howe by Ayton Smithy. A climb followed and thence over the Bowstring girder bridge, impressive by its isolation, and so to Luthrie Station which had despatched many an agricultural ton in its short life span.

And so to Lindores where the glories of the sunset were painting the sky in the direction of the hidden Tay. We crossed the second Bowstring girder spanning the road from Lindores Loch and entered the cutting by historic Abdie, and on to Glenburnie Junction where stood the signalman ready to receive the tablet and possibly to switch out for another day: who knows?

We were on the final main-line stretch now beneath the brooding andesite cliff of old Clatchard with the volcanic waves of trap unseen, above. The beauty of the Tay and Mugdrum Island was as compulsively enchanting as ever and so we rolled on above the ancient town – belied by its name – to draw into Newburgh Station and there leave our 'Yorkie' (C15) to hie to Perth by Nechtan's Capital: Bridge of Earn and through the portal of Moncreiff tunnel to approach the Fair City.

Chapter 12

A Trades holiday journey with a thirsty fellow traveller

For the annual holiday of 1937, the whole family including an uncle from Glasgow and my aunt from Kirkcaldy decided to descend en masse on my Tayport aunt and uncle and to spend our holiday with them in response to their invitation.

The journey was, as always, by train from Kirkcaldy and was arranged for the first day of that year's Kirkcaldy Trades holiday. The trains, like the station, were crowded and finding a compartment for six of us was no simple exercise. When an appropriate compartment was located, it was in a corridor coach and I was banished to the corridor, on the basis, no doubt, that there I could be kept under the scrutiny of parental eyes. This vantage point suited me ideally, as my objective was to scrutinise, to the maximum, all aspects of the railway and its operation.

Some of the passengers had travelled from the south and a few were destined for beyond the Tay. By far the most interesting was a film technician – a very 'rare bird' to be found in that neck of the woods in these comparatively early days of the British film industry. He had a problem! He needed a drink and he needed it badly! My uncle commiserated with him. But – how to obtain such a commodity on the 11.28 a.m. Edinburgh to Dundee stopping train via Tayport on a Trades Holiday Saturday?

Thornton Junction was suggested as a faint possibility – possibly as a sop to ease his misery. The likelihood of such a proposition was speedily proved erroneous on arrival at the least exotic of all junctions. The next and only remaining possibility suggested was Ladybank as the existence of a refreshment room at that junction was postulated, it being implied that what in effect was the actual and original parting of the ways to Perth for the Highland Capital and Dundee for Aberdeen must merit the widest of facilities! For this traveller in a northern desert devoid of facilities (that the sophisticates of the home counties would regard as the fundamentals of civilised living) these two promised oases could not be reached one moment too quickly. But such was not to be! The line was packed with traffic – traffic that the beholders of the scene today could scarce imagine.

In the corridor, I surveyed the features of the passing scene with pleasurable enthusiasm, like that of some pilgrim *en route* to a long awaited shrine. Perhaps action, alas, was not the immediately operative word.

At Thornton South Junction, near the stained River Ore's ebony waters, where branched the spur to the western coalfields from Cardenden to Dunfermline and such Spartan realms beyond (Lochgelly, Lumphinans, Cowdenbeath, Kelty, *et al.*) we rumbled down the grade to a dead stand. All 'boards' on the soaring twin lattices were unmistakably horizontal. Ahead the diverging lines and sidings were alive with carriages, wagons and engines aplenty.

The fireman left his engine and made his way to the signal box, where he climbed the steps and disappeared within. Some time later he emerged, returned to his engine and pulled himself on to the footplate. (I was having a practical demonstration of rule 55 in operation.) A few parching minutes later the signal fell and we rolled up to the tortured and distorted platform, from beneath which the rich but shallow seams were being stripped.

The LNER, having rejected the ransom set on sterilisation, had demolished the original structures and had erected a host of sturdy timber replacements in their place.

More of the thirsty film-maker

Perhaps the parched traveller may have thought for a moment, on beholding the platform scene, that he was back on the set of a Western, with the saloon ready to assuage his raging thirst from within its stout timber confines. If so, reality speedily returned as his dash across the much-levelled platform produced neither barman nor precious fluid.

At long last, on we 'rolled', having left behind those who sought the pleasures of the East Neuk to clamber in to their waiting train. On past the large station signal box with its hidden array of levers (one hundred at its peak and two signalmen per shift), we rolled, to start our climb past Balgonie Colliery with its twin bings, twin chimneys, brick-kilns and a welter of surface-plant and machinery spreading east to the Leven Branch which curved away to that airt (and rising beyond which spread the 'Wemyss Firs', of many a boyhood excursion, and the remains of Earlseat Mines).

Further right there could be snatched the merest glimpse of the far distant Forth through a rural region en-mixed with mining symbols.

Upwards, climbing steadily to the cutting-hidden summit we progressed, only to dash briefly downwards, thereafter, to thread the lofty, arched viaduct across the Leven and stop at Markinch. From that platform-end, the climb was resumed to reach Lochmuir's Herron – favoured, moorland summit on the low eastern shoulder of the Lomond Range: the highest rail point betwixt Forth and Tay and favoured with signalbox and refuge siding.

Stops were a dominant feature of that train and such was called at Falkland Road (through which thunder the trains of today as they surge down to the spreading plain of the Howe). There was one further, maddening stop at Kingskettle's precariously-narrow, wooden platform perched atop its embankment and bridge and then Ladybank at last!

Hardly had we fully stopped, when, missile-wise, shot the victim of the consuming thirst, and sought the refreshment chambers so long awaited. Would the train crew allow sufficient drinking time, I pondered? Back he flew, and threw himself into the compartment – unsatiated, it appeared. The blessings of the can had yet to arrive! But what of the 'screw top'? Memory fails on these essential details. Dundee must now be the vital source of hope!

So on we went past the 'road to the north': the little loco-shed of grey-stone and leaded windows beside its attendant coaling stage where 'muscle ruled ok'.

Curving heavily now, with the engineers' domain on our right, we reached the forested acres of Ann's Muir and a view eastward to the high ridges of the Cults Lime Hills.

Soon came yet another stop (Springfield this time) and then on we travelled with the Eden River and its pattern of lades in view, to reach the county town's demure station premises against a backdrop of towers, turrets and spreading rooftops beyond the goods yard and bordering linen factories.

16. Leuchars – a junction no more – in Scotrail days. The branch to Tayport ran straight ahead through the site occupied by the house with the tiled roof in the background. The down train is leaving for Dundee. (Photo: Author, c.1995)

Had our fellow traveller become philosophical, we wondered, as our train pulled out beneath the bridge? Even we had two more stops before we would alight at our destination; but to that the thirst victim must possibly add another three – poor man! Dairsie was reached and left behind, and soon thereafter all the familiar landmarks were joyfully noted and an approaching end to the journey confirmed. Lo! at last we were drawing into Leuchars Junction.

Now it was our party's turn to suffer doubts. Someone suggested that on a Saturday one had to change for Tayport. Another seemed to remember having had to do so on some half-forgotten occasion. A porter was summoned and he quickly dispersed all fears.

Gasps of relief escaped all round. Only the film-maker remained morose. That once-dashing exponent of film technology despaired. Even in great screen epics, the villains are seldom subjected to such torment as this, he thought. But, then, he had not been aware of the hazards of travel in North Britain.

My heart leapt up to behold all the old familiar sights, tokens as they were of a rapidly impending end to our travels. To the right, lay the 'mill of the three chimneys', to the east the quaint church tower, whilst now we were passing the north junction signal-box. That curious anachronism, Leuchars Old Station, lay just ahead, and the signal box-controlled crossing just ahead of that.

Now we were running alongside the stand of tall trees with a wide forest spreading dark, beyond away to the hidden sea. The Rhynd Crossing was to follow and, after passage through a forest fringe, that enchanted moment when, of a sudden, the estuary swung into sight with Buddon Lighthouse, Lucky Scaup Tower/ Folly? and a captivating waste of blue waters.

Shortly followed the soaring chimney of the jute mill with the sheds and offices spreading from its base, then the green sweep of the golf course with the 'Mill Houses' on its fringe... then a huddle of factories to the left and the East Common to the right.

This brought us to yet another crossing (controlled by the immediately adjacent Tayport South Box) close to which crouched the gasworks, its ragged chimney of square section and its gasometer. Beyond that; the track was gauntletted by the saw mill and its capacious wood-yards spreading toward the harbour sidings (so often packed with wagons of coal and esparto grass).

The ancient coal-hoist of Tayport Harbour was now appearing, with a glimpse of the harbour beyond. But we rolled to a stop at the 'outer home' and had time to look forward to a railway panorama of engine-shed and sidings, abutted by the foundry with its cupola and red-brick core-stove-chimney.

There to the left leaned the venerable spire of the Parish Kirk, against a grey, town backcloth rising toward Spiershill and Scotscraig (far to the south-west) and intersected by lanes and narrow streets.

Truly, the fringes of the promised land were well in sight!

The signal dropped and, in ritual fashion, we drew in to that oft-remembered platform, in earnest anticipation of a week of interest and new experience that stretched ahead (and with the enthusiasm which is a benison of early years).

Chapter 13

Across the Border: drama at Preston; Southport delights and a Blackpool panacea

The ultimate journey would, I reckoned, be that which crossed the English border; but the prospects of that seemed slight. To my surprise and delight, however, my parents decided, in 1935, to have a week's holiday in Southport and so arose an opportunity to fulfil my ambition.

The Saturday of departure stands out clearly in memory. It commenced with a conventional journey to Edinburgh, where we left our train at Haymarket station and made our way to the LMS station at Princes Street, with its impressive arched roof and imposing hotel-frontage. There we joined a train whose coaches were distinctly different, not only in colour but in a variety of subtle variations in their internal decor, upholstery and furnishings.

My obsessive interest in the early portion of the journey was in achieving a border crossing and I must have tried my parents' patience by enquiring at virtually every station after Carstairs whether England had been entered. I certainly recall repeating the question at Symington, and further recall that it was raining there and that little rivulets were descending behind the sodden platform.

At Carlisle a change of trains was decreed, but though duly impressed by the scale of the station, my whole objective was to get on to the correct train for the next portion of the southward journey and to avoid detachment from my parents in the process. Because of this salient imperative, my lack of any formal locomotive knowledge and the general and somewhat alarming stir around me, the great potential to expand my locomotive observations was, miserably, dissipated. Our wait in that border station and strategic point of coalescence for so many routes was short, and we were soon aboard another impressive train.

I recall that the other occupants of our compartment were two single, middle-aged 'engineers' from Kilmarnock (turners, I think they told my father they were, with Glenfield and Kennedy), and they seemed set on putting engineering issues well behind them whilst they set about enjoying life to the full. Liverpool was the destination which I recall them to have quoted; perhaps, more likely, it would have been Blackpool! At any rate, all of us were destined for Preston for our next change of train.

At this point, I established myself in the corridor, where scope for scrutiny of the passing scene was much greater. In no time, I graduated to the window and thrust my head out, regardless of a hail of cinders. There remains a strong recollection of stopping at a junction with a terrace of unusual houses, which I assumed to be railway dwellings as there were railway facilities all round. A small tank engine positioned itself behind the train and when we started off, it was obviously banking us up an incline, which I now know to be Shap, and the railway depot Tebay.

Many years later, I recognised that terrace quite distinctly from a passing train. As we climbed, I watched the little tank engine intently and at the top there was a blast from its whistle as its driver shut off and we drew ahead of it. As it did so, its driver gave me a hearty wave, which I returned enthusiastically.

Preston station, I recall as the locus of a great milling multitude. Standing back from our train on alighting, we suddenly became aware of a great stir. Dashing through the crowd and scattering its constituents came a running figure, headed for the southbound train. Behind him followed a woman, running to overtake him but faltering in the attempt. The front runner positioned himself opposite an open door, at a coach extremity above the bogie, with his follower desperately attempting to duplicate the leap which the pursued was obviously contemplating. With a swing, the man leaped aboard the accelerating train but his sorely flagging pursuer made one final desperate attempt to catch him.

By this time numerous whistles were shrilling and there were howls of warning and gasps from the onlookers. Station staff were running now to dissuade her. Suddenly she seemed to summon up a final residue of strength and with a leap – or a stumble – propelled herself into the coach vestibule with not a movement of assistance from her companion. However, her legs dangled over the running boards and the onlookers anticipated the worst. One railway man, with a superhuman effort, thrust her legs into the vestibule as the train continued to accelerate down the platform with her figure on the floor of the coach and not a sign of her companion. No time to study locos with all this action in progress!

The Southport train was a much humbler affair than its two predecessors and was not a corridor train. The intermediate terrain has left the impression of a flat green expanse with a series of small stations with milk churns and general luggage, at all of which we stopped. I recall the lower-quadrant signals as being different also and in some way similar to old Caley signal equipment.

On we trundled (slowly, I thought) until the respectable confines of a station with an overall roof was reached and, suitably encumbered with luggage, we sought a taxi, the driver of which made a strategically circuitous journey to our boarding house. We were not to use the train for another week but many pleasant recollections remain, including hours in the pleasure gardens and sea-less beach or in the Hesketh Park, not to mention watching humbugs and associated products being manufactured by much pounding and stretching in a Lord Street window (a combination of education and anticipation or exquisite torture, one might say).

We also travelled by road, going by Liverpool, the first

Mersey tunnel and Birkenhead, to visit Port Sunlight and be conducted through all departments of a soapworks and receive on leaving a tablet with an imprint of the *Queen Mary* thereon. In addition, Chester was visited by road; and a sail taken on the Dee, after walking along the ancient wall.

Another day we went to Blackpool. The salient memory of this was not of the Tower but of an open-fronted booth, before which a small crowd milled round a man who had a snake coiled round his neck and who lectured with considerable animation. He was holding forth on the greatest panacea of all time, which by his general drift was guaranteed to cure all afflictions from the common cold to the black death; from syphilis to tuberculosis and cancer (the last, no doubt, after a repeat dose). All the crowned heads of Europe had sought out this incredible cure and he had had ineffable pleasure in passing the wonder drug to them (personally it was implied). Never had there been provided such an amazing boon to mankind.

Slight movements in his audience and certain low murmurings suggested to him the appearance of sceptics and infidels, there. He was spurred to greater heights of oratory and declared sorrow and unbelief at the merest hint of such diabolically inept sentiments. Learned sources of all types and conditions were quoted. Any physician who cast doubts was a parvenu: an apostate and generally incompetent.

A fringe-group remained unconvinced and made their views forcibly known in harsh Glasgow accents. The great man was distressed by such inept remarks, expressed in the face of high scientific endorsement.

'Go!' he said in a loud voice, 'and eat your toffee apples and do not waste our time.'

Just then there was a violent movement at the entrance. A group of men, linking arms and swaying as to some inaudible tune, burst upon the group and called in loud, unmistakably Glasgow, voices: 'Oh! It's you, McKay! It's Yersel! See you at Mechan's Gate on Monday morning.'

Just then, to my great annoyance, my parents pulled me outside and no more revelations were heard from the mouth of the great man, and of that panacea, I heard no more.

My uncle who resided in Glasgow had heard of 'McKay' and would only chuckle when I sought to hear more of his magic.

Around 1949 I went to a Modern Homes Exhibition in the Kelvin Hall in Glasgow. And there, exhibiting an amazing labour-saving device, appeared to be the self-same provider of wonder drugs!

Chapter 14

By rail to Bellahouston for the Empire Exhibition of 1938

The school-time years prior to the outbreak of war in 1939 were crowned by one outstandingly exciting event in 1938, for that was the year of the Empire Exhibition in Bellahouston Park, Glasgow and, in consequence, the year in which I first visited that city. Various groups organised visits to the exhibition and this practice was taken up by the employees of the workshop in which my father was employed, who arranged an excursion by rail.

The prospect of this trip excited me considerably, especially as the journey was to be by rail and would, perhaps, give me the opportunity to view the great enigma that for me was 'The Second City'.

It is doubtful whether such a prospect, if presented today, would generate much excitement in those of the equivalent age group. World-wide spectacles they no doubt view regularly and with equanimity, from the comfort of their own domestic environs. They are endowed with an ever-open window on the world and such a visit as this would secure a mildly interesting rating; or at worst be categorised as a 'non-event'.

The eagerly-awaited day dawned as one of somewhat uncertain prospect; but enthusiasm was too great to allow mere changeable weather to dampen our ardour as we stood in an expectant bunch at the end of Sinclairtown station's southbound platform. Soon we had found places in a corridor coach, and off we set along a now-familiar track by the coastal regions of the Forth.

Across the Forth we went and swung off to the west at Dalmeny, to pass through the shale field fringes of Winchburgh and Philipstown. Polmont was passed, and we then steamed through the murk of Falkirk tunnel, to emerge far above and away from the town which today sprawls upward to the lineside, where isolated brick tenements then stood as housing, no doubt, for colliers and perhaps for brick makers or moulders.

The Union Canal, whose tow path ran in parallel to the south of our route, now descended beneath us below a fine viaduct, and in a little time we were forging through the brickfields of Stirlingshire to penetrate the Dunbartonshire and North Lanark coalfields, betokened by the lineside collieries of Dullatur and Croy as well as those of Gartshore and Waterside (with Auchengeich slightly to the south) – all still very active.

From Waterside we passed to Garngaber and Lenzie and suddenly Bishopbriggs was upon us, as a manifestation of one of these familiarly named locations, which we were about to encounter. So, through impressive cuttings and past

17. The 'Turkey' yard to the left of Glasgow City Union Railway. Cowlairs junction in background and Sighthill yard goods line between. (Photo: Springburn Museum Trust)

Eastfield running sheds, with many an engine in sight, we steamed.

But there, past triangular junctions, we curved perceptibly to the left, to take the route of the old Glasgow City Union Railway (skirting the Turkey sidings and Springburn). Here now was Barnhill; and the familiar names were coming fast. Through a tunnel we plunged, to run close below Blochairn Steelworks, and past Alexandra Parade, Duke Street and Bellgrove (all grand-sounding names, thought I) to stop at St John's – right in the heart of the city and alongside the maze of tracks that fed High Street goods station to the left.

By now, the sheer vastness of the city had, already, become apparent.

So, by LMS metals, and, no doubt, with a 'Soo West' crew, we soon crossed the Clyde by an impressive viaduct of elaborate red stone abutments, and eventually reached a special station updated for the event at Bellahouston.

The memory of that exhibition remains indelible, but that is another tale. Suffice to say, that engineering in all its facets was widely displayed. Many west-coast firms, such as the Beardmore conglomerate, had their own stands, in their case displaying, amidst other products, a marine crankshaft of eye-catching proportions (which one of my latter day turner-instructors and former Beardmore turner, in an illusion-shattering moment, advised me had been of wood!). Many were the models of an astounding excellence and detail, by which the Clydeside output was impressively represented.

One stand was that of the British Aluminium Company, who were attracting the junior ranks of visitors with a small acorn or egg of aluminium, sitting in an aluminium 'egg-cup' or retainer and attached to it by a string, the object being to eject the 'egg' from its perfectly fitting container and catch it thereafter in its original relation. These toys were being swallowed up as popular souvenirs.

The Dominion Pavilions stand out in memory: Canada,

18. Tait's Tower: Empire Exhibition, Glasgow 1938. (Valentine's 'Art Colour' postcard, postmarked June 1938)

South Africa and Burma in particular (for reasons no longer clear).

Astounding and never to be forgotten was the joint railway companies' pavilion, whose central focus was a 'giant' model railway. A book-stall was also in operation and to this day (though now its binding doth protest after fifty-six years of handling) a copy of a GWR title, *Track Topics*, remains in my bookcase. Steel mills and mining were also represented effectively.

The Scottish Co-operative Societies were likewise well-represented and details of their manufacturing units at Shieldhall and elsewhere are clearly recalled. Tait's Tower, by its dominant position and striking lines, could in no manner be missed and there was regret (owing to its popularity, I seem to recall) that its summit was not explored. For me, it seemed truly to represent the future, with an idiom that impressed me personally as being synonymous with the ethos of 'Things to Come'; the challenging pages of the 'Modern Wonder' and the communal notions evolved by my chum and me as we discussed and re-discussed the marvels that science would bring in that 'inevitable' period indubitably ahead. How incredibly wrong we were and how sadly awry were our pathetic beliefs in man's ability to utilise scientific knowledge and develop it for the benefit of all mankind.

Engineering and industry were my consuming interests from the exhibition's cornucopia and I was not disappointed. Pathetically, I believed that such were the cardinal criteria of a nation's status and would be universally regarded as such by the community at large. But the dominance of the accountant had yet to dawn and perhaps, as Paul says, 'when as a child we see as a child'. Perhaps, in later life, we discern our interpretation as childlike?

I still recall the pavilion of the Church of Scotland and also the Highland clachan as strictly non-industrial aspects of Scottish life and earlier history, respectively.

By no means peripheral for a vast proportion of the visitors was the amusement park; but I regret to report that to that amazing sector we did not penetrate, weird as it may seem to many whose eye may light on these meanderings.

A major impression, however, was generated by the visitors themselves – by their numbers and their enthusiasm and, not least, by their wide divergence in age, class and type. There was also something of the city essence itself – of the energy and vitality and sheer sense of life in all its myriad facets.

There was also a city icon, as it were, at one boundary point where the later-to-be-familiar tenements, in the authentic red sandstone, peeped over the exhibition's periphery.

Round the exhibits, along spacious 'roads' and up the steeper tree-lined ascents, plied a fleet of small mobile 'platforms' endowed with seats (or forms) and powered by sturdy little internal-combustion-engined tractors of compact and robust design (by Lister of Dursley, Gloucester) which conveyed the more weary or foot-sore but perfervid visitors.

In later years I was to witness these at close range, though then they had been metamorphosed into industrial workhorses. Even later still I observed descendants or derivatives in locomotive form pulling ash and lime, prodigiously.

Above the Gorbals, by the City Union Railway, Gallowgate station and Haghill to glimpse Hyde Park

The dominant impression from that most memorable day was that of the homeward journey.

We left in mid evening, after waiting some time on the platform, deserted other than for our own group, in a murky light which seemed initially to presage rain.

I scanned the line to the west for some indication of our train. In due course, through the cloud there were signs of engine exhaust and beneath the gloom the dull profile of a locomotive heading a train of coaching stock. There followed the pleasing boom of a Caley whistle. Sadly there is no precision to my definition of the engine type, though I do recall a 'cut-a-way' cab of a Drummond touch; and reflection suggests a Caley 'Jumbo'.

Off we set through the southern suburbs and were soon creeping aloft through the old Gorbals, with its incredible labyrinth of tenements, warehouses and factory premises. As we crept along, the evening magic was creeping in to the sky and expelling to lower depths the earlier unrelieved murk. As it diffused, it added its essential element to the magic of a great city by night.

Across the Clyde we went, with the vista of Clyde Street and its bustle, and swept across the Saltmarket with a commanding view of Glasgow Cross, dominated by its steeple, and the

Trongate, with all the stir and bustle of that busy city-centre thoroughfare.

There it was – the great enigma! – after all these years of envisaging, coming to life before my eyes and more fascinating than fancy!

We stopped in a deserted station, dark, remote and mysterious, identified some time later as the old Gallowgate Station of the City Union Railway, abandoned when the electric tramcars spelt the end of the St Enoch's to Springburn service around 1904. All around lay dark, mysterious buildings, some in silhouette from the bright lighting of a dynamic city. On again we went, re-engined, through the yards of St John's and by tunnels to Bellgrove.

Through Haghill Junction, through a tenement swathe, we went, to rumble through buttressed cuttings below the lowering mass of Blochairn Steelworks with its forest of chimneys – not one brick of which structure now remains upon another. We surfaced through a deserted Barnhill, before which the busy goods junctions diverged and to the left of which spread the multiple lines of Sighthill, with every evidence of rail-borne merchandise and diverse freight.

To the right sprawled the Atlas Works, of which no vestige now remains. Simultaneously to the left there spread a towering mass of workshops, of indistinct detail in the evening shadow; and, behold! a snaking line of magnificently painted locomotives projecting through an arch proclaiming on its metal surface 'Hyde Park Works'. There could be little doubt that we were threading the mazes of Glasgow's railway suburb – with four major locomotive plants, cable works and steel re-rolling mills.

And so to Fife, through the gathering dusk of a fine summer's evening, after one never-to-be-forgotten day: little realising that one day there would be a return and the fulfilment of the desire to learn of the many faces of that unique and warm-hearted city, whose heyday has gone but whose memory will long remain in many a quarter.

CHAPTER 15

Railway byways in Perthshire; a Sentinel railcar to Methven; LNER Sentinel railcar sightings at Dysart! and Ladybank

There was one recurrent, though less frequent, journey which in early years provided travel over less familiar routes. This was to the small Perthshire village of Methven to which, it transpired, my great-grandmother's brother and wife had retired after many years in Dumbarton. There also resided his niece and several friends and acquaintances. In that village my family had, in consequence, a small group of friends of many years standing.

Methven lies a few miles to the west of Perth and was on a short branch from the Perth to Crieff (via Almondbank) line. In early days the village was served by a station on the Crieff railway – as I had often been told by my relatives – but at a later

19. Methven station in Caledonian days. (Reid postcard, c.1902, postmarked 18 April 1905)

stage a short branch line of 1 mile 308 yards in length had brought the benefits of the railway to a small terminus on the southern fringe of the village, complete with goods depot and engine shed. Copies of a coloured postcard remain, showing the platform and shed with a Caley tank engine standing outside the latter. The distance by rail from Perth to the terminus was possibly around 6.15 miles or so.

Our journey was usually made from Tayport during a holiday stay at that spot and so embraced three sub-journeys, viz: the very familiar and intensely used ex-NBR, Tayport to Dundee line via Wormit and the Tay Bridge; the ex-Caley main-line from Dundee (West) to Perth; and the ex-Caley route to Methven (utilising the joint main line to Inveralmond, the Crieff line via Almondbank to Methven Junction and then the short branch to Methven terminus).

The more stimulating sections were those from the West station along the Carse of Gowrie at an expected and glorious mile-a-minute timing (a haunt of Caley No. 123 in the mid twenties I have been told).

There one could view these unmistakable Caley lower-quadrant signals by thc lineside, as well as their typical wayside stations, and revel in the sheer beauty of the immediately adjacent river Tay, making its deep seaward course between its lush banks somewhere west of Glencarse and before the curving bridge across the Tay (and curious Moncrieff Island) whose approach was heralded by Barnhill Box and a slowing for tablet exchange.

Beyond the bridge and close to its abutment stood the fascinating waterworks building, unmistakable by its dome and obelisk-like chimney and carved inscription. (Memory may have defaulted – but I seem to recall *Aqua et Igne Haurio* as the text.)

The large Douglas and Grant vertical engine was not, however, visible from the train, housed as it was in its equally impressive, generously fenestrated, ashlar-built stone engine-house. An elevated section followed to Princes Street Station, in effect a ticket platform for the open-station operation of Perth General Station, at whose perceptibly curved 'Dundee' platform we then de-trained.

A walk of great potential interest followed across bridges and platforms to locate the Methven train with the ever-present hope of sighting interesting locomotives of the LMS stud.

I recall the desired platform lying to the north-west of the station complex and taking the form of a dock platform. The Methven train was made up of but few coaches and was locomotive-hauled in the early days. In the middle thirties, however, as I recall matters, a Sentinel Railcar was brought into service. A return journey in this vehicle I certainly do recall: the fireman remaining behind to tend the vertical boiler and the driver going forward to the leading cab. I remember the line-side features of both up and down journeys but, as the ultimate journey was in the 'up' direction, it is the detail of that journey that remains most distinct.

On that occasion there was certainly no change at Methven Junction. The tall station-building at Almondbank had platform access in its lower regions and road access at high level. The line curved to the right on leaving that station, and entered a short cutting, at the inlet end of which a freight siding branched to feed a bleachfield. I recall, if memory is accurate, that this was owned by Lumsden and MacKenzie, whose steam wagons, I also recall passing through Glen Farg when on some of our many safaris to that wooded pass in the days of the original, much-used road to the Beinn Inn and the south. I seem to recall the siding being electrified with an overhead catenary and operated by a small electric locomotive.

There was a brick chimney there, of medium height, and the siding wound into an open doorway in the indistinct regions beyond which faint electric lighting could be discerned.

Further up from the main line, the Tulloch works of Messrs Pullar could be seen not far from the line-side (though possibly closed not long before: I vaguely remember reading that this in its time was the largest dry-cleaning unit in the country and had a spirit-tank of vast proportions).

Around Perth, in those days, there was always great railway activity to catch the eye. A feature of travel into Perth on such lines was a stop at Muirton Platform, where, as at Princes Street and Bridge of Earn, tickets were uplifted, to maintain the open station status at the main station. My last experience of this process came some years later when I made my last journey on the Crieff line by catching the 6.06 p.m. train from Crieff via Almondbank, but by then the passenger branch from Methven Junction had gone (that being July 1951).

I was never fortunate enough to make the through journey from Perth to Balquidder (as I would have loved to have done) nor even the journey from Crieff to Gleneagles via Highlandman, Muthill, etc. Work at all times dominated the programme and when its influence eventually diminished, many years later, these delectable railway byways had long since seen their last train. There was one minor exception, however, as in the sixties a pilgrimage was made by car to Crieff and a photograph made of a class-five-headed train snaking over the junction of the Almondbank and Gleneagles lines to branch off and disappear towards Highlandman and Muthill and its destination of Gleneagles Junction.

Nor did I ever travel on the Caledonian Railway branch line from Strathord (near Luncarty) to Bankfoot; but I have a very clear recollection of a car excursion from Tayport in the thirties when our route brought us alongside the Bankfoot Light Railway (where we ran for some distance alongside a light engine, no doubt making its way to Bankfoot). My knowledge then of locomotives was too inadequate to allow exact identification, but in retrospect I am of the opinion that the tank engine seen then was that of Caley design. Alas, greater precision cannot be had! Sixty years seems an unbridgeable gap for any detailed memory check.

My last fragile recollection of the line to Balquidder is possibly a recollection scarcely worthy of record. One autumn weekend in the eighties, a group of companions took a caravan to Lochearnside, and on an afternoon of uncertain weather we set about scaling the northern slopes by the loch. Suffice to say that the winds blew at full strength and the rain descended in monsoon proportions. On the downward path we crossed a fence to find a well-defined and level track, whose wooded fringes offered marginally improved protection from the unceasing downpour. How regular this enclave seemed in all this water-logged wilderness! It was no other than a fragment of the abandoned railway from St Fillans to Balquidder. What a fair prospect that must have been, before the trackside woods achieved their present height!

The Sentinel steam railcar made its last run to Methven in the autumn of 1937. Generally, the Sentinel railcars seem to have had short operational lives on their respective branches and such was the fate of that nearer to my home, in Fife. An LNER variant of the design operated between Thornton and Methil via West Wemyss, Wemyss Castle and Buckhaven, but this was eventually supplanted by locomotive haulage on the branch (a task eventually allocated to a C15 non-superheated 4-4-2 tank engine of NBR Reid design). The usual problem on such branches was the inevitable and ultimate need to pull a goods van or additional passenger coach/coaches.

An early recollection is of seeing the Sentinel unit in question running toward Dysart Station one Saturday morning around 11.45 a.m. (*c.*1934?) to some unknown destination. Such a strange sighting was never repeated or in any way explained. There is a faint recollection of seeing a similar unit in the dock at Ladybank Station (perhaps about to do duty on the Mawcarse Branch) but details of this fleeting memory are nil. The LNER unit was painted in light green and cream colours, I seem to recall, and the overall effect seemed to give a much lighter, cleaner appearance than that of the LMS unit, which seemed to have a somehow sombre appearance, if faint memories are to be accorded credibility for such comparison.

Chapter 16

By rail to Perth in 1938; an aerial view of an aerial ropeway and a 'Scott' monument

One year later I went on a further memorable rail-journey. The time was again the summer Trades week; and the destination, on this occasion, was a more ambitious one – to the 'Highland Capital'.

The Saturday morning of that week saw the same band as that of the previous year, lined up on the north-bound platform of Kirkcaldy station, watching a procession of trains, many of them 'holiday specials' moving south and north (a delectable spectacle for an observer of locomotives). Eventually, in rolled our 'special' with its Perth headboard, which was to convey us to Perth, direct via Ladybank and Newburgh – a most acceptable journey as it was by a less-accustomed route, although not one that was by any means totally unknown.

The most intense recall is of the elevated section of line from beyond Glenburnie Junction, commencing with the fine stone arch above that hamlet (now signposted as Den of Lindores, though never known to me as such in my schooldays). Immediately thereafter was the siding for Mare's Craig Quarry where the aerial ropeway had inspired boyhood wonder. This was now viewed from above and at its termination rather than beneath its initial sector.

Then came the curving crawl below the towering face of Clatchard Crag which allowed a full appreciation of those breathtaking river vistas to the reed-beds of Mugdrum Island and those of the Carse (of Gowrie) beyond, so often seen and admired from the 'North of Fife' train in early mornings of old.

Newburgh was soon upon us and there was the foot-bridge to 'Jacob's Ladder', an early, minor obstacle in the race to Clatchard's fortress-crowned summit on other holidays. To its right spread the dwellings of Mountpleasant. Beyond this point the long orchards behind the High Street dwellings were spied upon, in 'nosey-parker' fashion.

Hill Street Bridge was now being traversed and beyond that, I knew, lay the screens of Robertson's quarry, which had become of interest after the sighting of a steam traction engine close thereto, some years before. We were moving slowly now, through the site of the original station (which had been burned down many years before) and in no time were edging through the new station with the oft regarded billboard with the likeness of Sir Walter Scott's Monument constructed from marmalade-filled jars by the eponymous preserve makers of Carluke.

To me, the Newburgh station complex always appeared the trimmest of passenger plus goods stations, though to passengers its location was sadly inconvenient for a town set on a steep hill and the least able to withstand the ferocious competition of the fast-growing bus companies.

Over the Fife border, into Perthshire and through Abernethy we now steamed; and running through the latter station, the opportunity was taken to spy the Round Tower from this unusual angle.

Thence we steamed across the plain to Bridge of Earn (where the LNE from Edinburgh via Glenfarg and the LMS from Glasgow via Stirling converged). There, we stopped, possibly for ticket-checking purposes.

At that point we entered the portals of Moncreiff tunnel, whose gloom was intensified by its deep rock cutting approaches, and from whose ventilation shaft engine-exhausts had shot skywards, like the venting of some latter-day Scottish volcano – as I had watched with fascination, in earlier days, from the adjacent roadway. My mother had described her impression of its length on journeys as a girl (in local non-corridor trains) and this impression was that day confirmed.

Emerging into the daylight, Friarton yards were seen and the LNER shed passed. Stationary, without, I seem to recall, a C15 (perhaps my early morning loco 9004 of the 'North Fife' journeys in earlier days) and a 'Scott' (from the small complement of LNER locos standing at that small, stone-built structure).

Soon thereafter, we rolled under St Leonard's bridge (a spotter's paradise of later times?) and entered the impressive confines of Perth General Station.

Perth General station

Perth Station had always seemed an awesome place to me, possibly because of the proliferation and length of its platforms; the impressive stonework of its imposing offices; its spreading and soaring roof and, above all, the constant bustle of its interior generated by long distance trains to appealing destinations (ripe for exploration in some far away undefined and remote future); freight trains were glimpsed in distant, station-avoiding regions as well as much shunting of coaching stock from and to equally remote regions of this formidable spread of rail activity.

As a by-product, there was the prime opportunity to view a wide range of locomotives, many of an unfamiliar if not totally unknown nature, such as the Caley locomotive element of the LMSR (an institution seemingly very different across the spectrum from the LNER).

Old Caledonian engines were a source of some irritation in that , unlike their counterparts in the LNER stock, their cab-side numbers were hard to define, being prolific in digits, congested and generally indecipherable, especially if viewed from some inauspicious vantage point (such as would be enforced if the engine was standing on the bridge beyond the Dundee platform and the viewing position was in the external station yard, then used as a general bus terminal).

Our connecting train was advised as being up to the north-west of the station and so involved an apparently extended journey across the manifestations of the foot-bridge and along a lengthy platform. As ever, much bustling activity was encountered *en route*: trains arrived and left; late passengers made unaccustomed darts and swerved and wheeled to avoid other knots of timeous travellers. Inevitably whistles shrilled and there was the usual cacophony of buffer blows; the screech of wheel on rail in unidentified lyes; the trundle of laden trolleys and sundry calls or yells from harassed staff or anxious passengers. All of this engendered a general air of excitement, wonder and perhaps mild apprehension.

In due course our connecting train was identified and proved to be located in the north-west quarter of the station. It was a lengthy one. A suitable compartment was sought out (not the most simple of tasks on that Saturday of intense traffic); but, in due course, the party were suitably ensconced. This process, I endeavoured to sustain patiently, though, in reality, I was keen to be off, since the prospect of a safari through largely unknown territory – as in the southern expedition of some years previous – was creating the antithesis of patience.

Aboard the Highland Express and Inverness-bound; I evaluate the LMSR

Impatiently, I endured the flurry of comings and goings in our carriage and in the train generally. As in our southern journey of several years back, our train had the indefinable atmosphere of a train of importance (bound, it seemed, for a destination and route sought out by those of distinction and by 'professional travellers').

No rustic 'dawdler', this, but a genuine express bound for a 'capital' and, by the nature of the luggage being energetically stowed in the vans and the peremptory accents and unusual, if not eccentric, dress of the owners thereof, patronised by a 'superior' and well-travelled clientele, who were much less likely to pursue the more mundane features of Thornton or Springfield – thought I.

My uncle had once uttered a comment in my aghast presence which I considered as blasphemy.

'Engine drivers of the Caley,' he had opined, 'somehow look smarter and more august than those of the other lines,' including, I presumed, the LNER. Surely this must have been some unconsidered joke, in poor taste, I tried to convince myself. Perhaps this was a time to test for any highly unlikely element of actuality in this heretical concept.

I glanced around and peered up front towards our 'own' engine. There was so much different, in this station. Perhaps it was its size that made it seem so grand. But size, I argued (with strong NBR loyalties surging within) was not the ultimate criterion. In any case, was it not a 'joint' station? But these footplatemen did look smart; and I began to doubt. Their caps did seem more decorously worn and there seemed just a little less grime.

Well, thought I, loyal to the last; perhaps they have just started their shift. In any case, the LMS did not have all the advantages. Their coaching stock might seem grand, but it was too fussy. It did not have the good old 'lived-in' feel of the LNE stock provided for us Fifers, I reasoned.

There was something stimulating about this train and the present environs, though, I thought, but that was perhaps all to do with history and geography and was not solely the creation of the LMS organisation! This was going to be an exciting journey, I mused; but I would take some weaning-off the well loved, old LNER.

At last: the ultimate trunk had been loaded; the last passenger had scurried up the platform and pompously stepped aboard and the earlier continuous movement up and down the corridor was, at long last, at an end.

The last of a cacophony of whistles had sounded and from 'up front' a deep throated blast had boomed. Admit it never – but the LMS whistle note was pleasingly evocative!

There came, immediately, a controlled blast from the chimney top that reverberated in the spacious and cavernous hollows of the impressive roof and we were at long last indubitably moving up the lengthy platform.

In no time, thereafter, we left the station proper, but it was not a little time before we had escaped from Perth's railway domain and its seemingly interminable proliferation of sidings and sheds, warehouses, workshops, ticket-platforms, signalboxes and private lyes.

But Inveramond junction was eventually passed; the 'Bogle Brig' crossed; and the joint line to the north climbed towards Luncarty (with its impressive viaduct across the north-bound road) to gain – at last – Stanley Junction and the fork to Forfar, wide Strathmore and distant Aberdeen.

The long train seemed to steam confidently northwards, through pleasant woodlands, by Murthly way; towards the hazy blue of distant hills – and to our Highland destination beyond.

Limited knowledge of Highland geography now augmented

In years to come, I was to explore the Highland Line, south of Carr Bridge, fairly thoroughly; but at the time currently described, all of it to me was virtually virgin territory, in that year of 1938.

My aunt, who was a member of the party, had made frequent journeys to the Highland region around Laggan and also to a village contiguous to Inverness, where she had stayed with a friend of her school-days. She spoke in ecstatic terms of all things Highland, including specifically the pure, unsullied air, the majestic and glorious scenery, and the ways and speech of the Highlanders. Many a time she had retailed her enthusiasm for the region and had described her holiday experiences in these environs, which had provided so much happiness. Her tales had included the requisite journeys over the Highland Railway and the names of stations such as Kingussie and Aviemore were well known to me from many a repetition.

When very small, my brother, along with my mother, had accompanied my grandfather on an excursion by rail to Inverness and I had been deeply disappointed that I had not been allowed to accompany them. From thenceforward, a prime desire had been to emulate that memorable journey.

Again, in a pictorial section of my aunt's volumes of *The Children's Encyclopaedia* – to the study of which I was much given – there was featured a picture of two locomotives (with unmistakable Jones chimneys) deep-buried in drifts, from which extraction operations were in hand. This purported to indicate the winter conditions experienced on the Highland Line. (Interestingly, some recent publications have reprinted this old picture – with information as to the nature of the incident – but in early days it enhanced interest in that famous line. The scene in question has since been defined as snow-ploughing at Achterneed in December 1906.)

From these various references, remote and indirect as they were, I felt that I had some knowledge of the line, but – I regret to say – such was my limited knowledge of the geography of the region traversed that definition of the exact route was correspondingly somewhat vague. Certain isolated areas were known, however, as these had been explored in part by road, in excursions from very early holiday-bases at Newburgh and Tayport, the former by bus and the latter by car, in highly eventful safaris which are too colourful to be diverted to meantime. Suffice it to say for the moment, that Ballinluig (the junction for Aberfeldy and that delectable railway branch of happy memory) had been visited – an area well known to my parents and to my mother in particular (who spoke with feeling of the Braes of Tullimet and a little croft on their heights).

One glorious car exploit from Tayport had penetrated to Killiecrankie, where we had walked beneath the arches of Mitchell's noble viaduct to seek the Soldier's Leap.

Later years had seen car trips to Inchmagranachan where Black Fives in tandem would be observed pulling their expresses northward as they followed the fast flowing Tay; but (as with the combing of Pitlochry's rivers and gorges and the tracts around Aviemore), such joys were in a distant future and their respective regions as yet unknown.

Aviemore and Druimuachdar and Slochd Mhuich summits are passed; we enter Inverness backwards!

On, then, we steamed, through the unfailing beauties of Perthshire, which were to be increasingly sought out as the years advanced. The inevitably excellent vantage status of the corridor was sought, and eyes were feasted on the continuously unfolding scene. Many were the delights of the lush river-bank and the cloven, wooded ravine. Glimpsed through forest gaps were half-hidden romantic cottages, with that dormer style so redolent to me of the old Perthshire, some with timbered porches featuring knotted trunks as dual columns.

In that earlier foray south to Lancashire, the incessant guerdon had been the Border crossing. Here, it was immersion in the authentic Highland scene; though I was not sufficiently knowledgeable either to define or to recognise any specific boundary of this promised land featured in so many a panegyric from tales of my aunt.

The gorge of Killiecrankie swept in to view and soon its trim station proclaimed the advent of Blair Atholl. Gone, for the present, were the dense woodlands as we steamed through a notch in the moorland hills; up through Glen Garry, climbing palpably toward the dreaded Druimuachdar Summit.

Truly we must now be in the 'real' Highlands; and if confirmation of entry to the enchanted land was, indeed, required, it was promptly given by a passage through Dalwhinnie, with encores at Newtonmore and Kingussie. This must be the golden territory, so oft the subject of fervid recall, of which these names were in the chorus of that litany.

Inevitably Aviemore must soon be reached, I mused, and so it was, in all its unspoilt rudimentary functional form with no hint of the candyfloss monstrosity of the post-industrial age. In we drew to an active junction, with locomotives and rolling stock and a lengthy platform with all the stir, animation and ritual worthy of an urban station, but set in the paradox of these spreading fastnesses.

As we steamed out, I rejoiced in this indubitable arrival in the Highlands and scrutinised every feature of the rolling scene with increasing interest and fascination. To the north: Carr Bridge (of disaster infamy) was crossed and on we forged, ultimately to achieve Slochd Mhuich Summit (unmistakably identified by its lineside boards). Daviot had been another much-repeated name in the promised itinerary and this we, thereafter, passed.

It was, however, a token of the impending end to our journey, but surprisingly, for me, the character of the countryside appeared to grow milder and less 'Highland' of aspect (to my circumscribed concept of geography).

In time, far glimpses of the distant Moray Firth were caught and, later, increasing evidences of railway activity, in the form of sidings and yards and other unmistakable railway artefacts heralded a cautious approach to Inverness. To my surprise we appeared to be about to by-pass the arch-roofed station and head north on the hypotenuse of an impressive triangular set of junctions. But the chimney blast fell silent and on went the brakes.

In a moment or two, back we set, and rolled to a smooth stop within the station of the Highland capital.

Chapter 17

Monster Sightings; A Speyside railway and oscillation on the Gondolier

During our week's stay, Inverness and its environs were examined with the usual intensity of the family on holiday in a new venue. My father and my uncle were enthusiastic walkers and all members were keen to absorb the history and to visit the landmarks in the vicinity. The Ness banks and its islands were well explored; as was Tomnahurich, the wooded cemetery mound close by the Caledonian Canal, which waterway the Brahan Seer was said to have predicted in his uncanny way. Such were but a few of the forays on foot.

As I recall matters, Messrs Macrae and Dick were the pre-eminent providers of 'motorised' excursions to the adjacent sights and an opportunity was taken to avail ourselves of some of these trips.

Culloden battlefield was visited, as was Loch Ness, Castle Urqhuart and Drumnadrochit (where local monster sightings were retailed for the benefit of the 'tourists', one young lad being obviously and deeply hurt by his suspicion of a degree of scepticism in some of his hearers).

On one afternoon of sustained sunshine we went to Nairn. On another afternoon of generous identical conditions we 'toured' the indisputable natural beauties of Glen Affric (at that time threatened by a hydro-electric proposal).

On yet another afternoon the fine pine-woods of the Boat of Garten, Grantown-on-Spey and adjacent districts were explored and (for my part) this demanded exploration of the former GNSR line from Keith. Although not a major objective of the group, the track was stumbled on by chance in its glorious Speyside environs. No locomotives were that day in evidence, however. Indeed, it would be some twenty-eight years before I was to travel over its tracks, and behind a main-line diesel locomotive on surely the enthusiast's excursion supreme (from Edinburgh visiting Carlisle via the Waverley 'road'; Mossend; Larbert; Perth; Forfar; Aberdeen and Keith before reaching 'The Boat' and ultimately Aviemore and Stirling). But that tale is for some other time.

Nor could I have envisaged the creation of a new steam railway from a portion of its track-bed (over which I would one day travel). However, all of the above 'coach trips', interesting and instructive exercises as they proved to be, paled to insignificance in comparison with two major excursions, which included railway and mechanical sightings of significance (at least, such was my view!).

The first of these involved a sail from Clachnaharry locks at

20. PS Gondolier *at Caledonian Canal, Inverness. (Real Photographs Photocard, purchased 1938)*

Inverness to Fort Augustus, a bus journey to Fort William and a return by bus to Inverness.

Passengers were taken from a collection point in the town to the canal locks by Macbrayne's bus – and I well remember the horror my father expressed at the fare charged for this short journey. The vessel boarded, there was the PS *Gondolier* (which – I have been told – was sunk as a block ship at Scapa Flow during the war which was to follow some two years later). She was a trim little vessel maintained in immaculate fashion.

For me, the engine room was fascinating, as it contained an oscillating-cylinder design of steam engine, an arrangement which I had not encountered till then. Needless to say, I spent much of the voyage observing this machine in operation. My father recalled such an engine in operation in one of the smallest linoleum manufacturer's works in Kirkcaldy. The engine room was also immaculate, with not a steam leak in sight. Indeed, being a vertical engine, there was an unencumbered engine-room floor and to my total amazement this was largely covered with some form of carpeting. The engineer was somewhat elderly and extremely trim in appearance, devoid of any trace of grime. Young persons tend, however, to estimate age somewhat on the high side, and such may have been the case in this instance.

As always, the opportunity to sail was much appreciated whilst, in this case, it gave an ideal platform from which to survey Loch Ness and its environs.

An unsuccessful Highland railway project: an early and major industrial Hydro-Electric installation; NBR engines encountered at last

When Fort Augustus was reached, we steamed into the impressive locks which gave access to the next section of the Caledonian Canal and there it was that we had to bid goodbye to the sturdy 'Paddler', whose sponsons now dominated the lockside.

21. Fort Augustus with evidence of a rail track-bed. (Hartmann postcard)

Ashore, the mechanism of the locks and their impressively robust construction was duly inspected. An exploration on foot was made in the direction of what appeared to be a large, disused, sturdily-symmetrical bowstring-girder bridge, and the adjacent lands towards the lochside.

The environs of the Abbey were also viewed, as was the disused terminus of the Fort Augustus to Spean Bridge Railway. This had been the only operational or, indeed, completed, portion of a major Highland Railway Project to link Inverness with Glasgow (but which had been ultimately operated by the North British Railway (from 1st May 1907) and its successor the LNER as a branch from the West Highland Railway). Operation continued till 1911 and after a period of closure from 1st August 1913 till 1st December 1933.

The sad state of desuetude observed turned out, it later transpired, to be a temporary situation, as the branch was reopened in the war years as an effective means of timber haulage (alas, only to be finally abandoned in the early post-war period on 1st January 1947).

We presumed that the disused bridge was the only remaining artefact of the envisaged key section from Fort Augustus up the Great Glen to Inverness. Such a section was never constructed and this bridge led to the Loch Ness Pier Station operated by the Highland Railway at the initial opening in 1903 but never by the NBR, its successor on the branch. The bridge was dismantled for scrap in the Second War, as was a hand-operated bridge over the canal.

Of this line, I was to hear some lively yarns, which brought it all to life again for story-teller and listener alike; but that lay some eleven or so eventful years ahead.

After a thorough reconnoitre of the area (interspersed for me by some ferocious bouts of toothache) another Macbrayne bus was boarded, which took us by Spean Bridge and on to Fort William, with various sightings of the West Highland Line along the ultimate part of the way. This inspired some descriptive comments – or, more accurately, eulogies – from my uncle. He had made a series of sporadic pilgrimages from Glasgow to Mallaig and had fallen under the spell of that unique and beautiful railway. On a practical note, reference was made to Loch Trieg as a source of hydro power for the BA Co. at Fort William and to the works involved in constructing that supply and its effects on the railway and on the loch levels.

As I very vaguely recall, the small (narrow-gauge) railway built to convey constructional and maintenance materials could be discerned high up on the hillside, but in this case time has eroded memory severely and the recollection is too flimsy to be trustworthy.

In due time we drew in to Fort William and I was thrilled that a place which had so often been referred to in my uncle's week-end yarns (during his sporadic visits to his Fife roots) had at last materialised and was about to be entered.

A natural attraction was the pier, which to my great satisfaction was immediately adjacent to the railway station. Indeed, at that time the rail tracks extended through the station and ran parallel to the quayside. A Macbrayne steamer arrived and there was much stir and an air of excitement. This turned to elation and amazement when Lo! I beheld a clutch of engines (of which a Glen and a J37 I clearly recall).

An ubiquitous NBR profile at the Fort: first encounter with the red and black funnels in Loch Lhinne

For the first time, my railway and my Scottish geography started to coalesce, as I realised that these engines were of the same engine class that laboured back home in Fife. Somehow, naively, it seemed incredible to me that I should encounter these 'old friends' in a territory so vastly remote from home. How things have changed across the years! How Scotland and the world have dramatically contracted, as a consequence of changes in technology and in the resulting changes in social conditions. The spasm of wonder and excitement born of a nascent discovery is still recalled. Such true joys are denied the cynical old, it would seem.

I gazed down Loch Linnhe from whence had come the imposing steamer with the twin red and black funnels (from Oban, I presume) and admired the lochside scene and the undefinable aura of the West Highlands. Somehow the presence of a steamer or a locomotive, I mused, seemed to provide a catalyst to release the ultimate experience. Such a thought, in many a book, must be the ultimate blasphemy. For some reason, the Fort William area seemed to have a magic element that excelled all to date; perhaps I had been fatally indoctrinated by all these years of West Highland Line rhetoric.

It would be some years yet ere I glimpsed the White Sands of Morar, contemplated Ben Dorain as it rose behind the Horseshoe Curve, or marvelled at the innovative concrete of the Glenfinnan viaduct above Kinloch Shiel; but Fort William was a foretaste of that enchanted land, threaded by the line of railway from Craigendoran to Mallaig.

Perhaps – in a way – RLS had expressed one facet of these

sensations in his addressing of the relative merits of hopeful travel and arrival. In later years, I returned many times to Fort William and revelled in its atmosphere, although analysis defied any rational explanation for this affinity, I had grudgingly to admit. The seeds of the hope had been expertly sown in the formative years but 'The Fort's' surrounding reality of mountain, loch and glen had justified and metamorphosed that 'hope' and all the conjectured dreams from an East Coast boyhood.

Our time was strictly limited, however, and we had to seek out the returning bus which would take us through the Great Glen. So, after a rapid perusal of certain remaining features, we joined yet another facility of the spreading Macbrayne empire; for – as they say – 'The Earth belongs unto the Lord and all that it contains; except the West Highland Piers and they are all Macbrayne's,' and in the year 1938, it appeared that buses as well as boats and piers in that West Highland airt fell also within that excepted domain.

Strangely enough, intense, manifold and evocative as were the beauties and the glories of that route, it was not those that marked that peregrination in the memory but rather a mundane, squalidly human, roadside encounter in a remote hamlet, location un-noted, furth of Fort Augustus, with a steamy, crowded bus as a stage.

A civil engineering rebellion and Aqua Vitae impinge on the Innocent Abroad

Somewhere after Fort Augustus, the bus drew in to the nearside verge of the narrow road and stopped. As it did so, I was vaguely aware of a momentary shadow, as some projectile – or bundle – hurtled over the bus roof and fell by the wayside. Simultaneously, there appeared to erupt a 'stir' of some kind. Shouted remarks broke the drowsy calm. Heated, wrathful exhortations of a decidedly non religious nature in a patois beloved in our times by the working class (if such are of the genus portrayed by the 'with it' modern literati), certain specimens of this actual group, not a few of today's excited schoolgirls, and degenerate patricians, alike. Such expletives and epithets were seldom heard in public in the 'refined' circles of 1938.

All of this was literally and metaphorically above my head, as I intently studied the unfolding, roadside scene, or attempted to do so, in so far as the requisite level of consciousness was possible in the superheated atmosphere of the congested bus. From my position it was nigh impossible to achieve a 360 degree view of events in any case, as the bus had its full complement of passengers and did not provide the ultimate in visibility, as is provided by the modern coach. Needless to say my father and uncle had sized up the situation immediately and defined the portent of events.

Just then the bus door was thrown violently open and a man of pronouncedly robust physique and broad build, with a deep tan and 'scuffing' clothes, thrust himself into the vehicle. As he came, he continued to direct a stream of belligerent invective to a far-off unseen audience. As would, inevitably, happen, the only seat vacant was apparently that next to mine and for this he made instanter. I have concluded, after a multitude of tram and bus journeys in Glasgow, that there must be some content of my disposition or physiognomy that attracts the malcontents, the riotous, the sectarians of both camps during the marches of their opponents, the impecunious of all races, the underprivileged and the 'stocious' (male and female alike).

Down he plumped and turned to ensure that I received an authentic and unabridged version of the injustice heaped upon him. Had I been endowed with the experience of years to come, I would have identified the aroma of his breath as that of Aqua Vitae, as the rhymer Robert Ferguson names it.

For a little time, he rumbled and rambled but soon subsided into personal musings, in a low key, no doubt under the influence of the numbing ambient of a congested bus and the ultimate effects of 'the Cratur'.

Symbols of an unknown world cast a transient shadow

This incident provided a marked discontinuity in an afternoon of pleasure and relaxation, injecting into the escapist element of the holiday a resurgence of harsh and unpleasant reality. For me it confirmed a growing concept of a dual world of contrast where the ever present harshness and ugliness were liable to erupt through a thin membrane of deceptive placidity and stability. Above was pleasure, beauty, accord, reason, equity and justice; but below lurked and seethed discomfort, ugliness, discord, chaos, prejudice and injustice. The sinister aspect of this seemed to be the timing of these intrusions from the negative region which were liable to arise when conditions seemed more pleasing and settled.

Over the journey, and from overheard discussions later, I pieced together the tale. My newly acquired neighbour was an Irishman who had been a ganger or sub-ganger on a large Civil Engineering Project (of which the Highlands had seen many and in post war years to come were to see many more). He had been an NCO in a Scottish Regiment of the British Army and had seen several years service. He had been on his last site for some time but had disagreed with the site agent and believed himself to be the victim of a serious injustice, the details of which, if known at the time, would no doubt be uncomprehended by inexperience and in any case are long since forgotten. He had 'chucked up' the job and walked off the site (after telling the agent, no doubt, what he thought of him, his site-abilities, his sense of justice, his firm, generally, their conditions of employment and the job). The projectile which had flown over the bus had been his overalls as a final gesture of disgust.

The world in which he lived and worked was at that stage totally unknown – indeed inconceivable – to me and possibly, had I known, repugnant and certainly challenging. Like so many others of these self-imagined or self defined challenges stored away in the memory, this was one more condition or task to be explored head-on and evaluated and for the chance of that full evaluation of typical site conditions, I had to wait till the very end of my working days for some opportunity to make some attempt at peripheral assessment (some fifty odd years up the line of life).

Perhaps emotion – even in a Fifer – is allowable in one's younger days. Possibly I had a slight excess, and in early days was unduly moved by hardship and suffering. When this was overcome, I believe that I became as a result harder and less sensitive than associates. In infant days I had a dread of death, possibly, I have postulated, as a consequence at a very early age of a severe and, I suspect, near-fatal bout of diphtheria. Implications of segregation or separation also worried me, in childhood days. One dread recollection from early childhood was of being on a Kirkcaldy tram when a child impaled on a cast iron spike was brought in by two workmen in their filthy working garments and restrained in the seat opposite until the stop was reached at the cottage hospital, while it screamed unceasingly in agony. That left a profound impression.

Nor was my home region in the twenties and thirties devoid of tales of accident and separation – but these do not concern this narrative. Suffice it to say that I felt sorry for my new 'companion' and a notion that the world was very much more than happy holidays with friends cast a transient cloud over the afternoon.

The Kyle train

As we rattled along the rustic roads, he continued to mutter away – whether to himself or to me, I now remember not. Near Inverness he got off, and as he rose, he patted me on the shoulder and, from a pocket, produced a collection of small change, which he insisted on my taking. This made a powerful impression on me. Not least, though not in a coherently ordered way, this made me muse on the world of work, where life was obviously hard, cruel, and demanded a depth of case-hardening, which I had not yet acquired. Lots of guts were obviously essential and I was decidedly unsure as to whether I had a sufficient quota. Acquisition of such might be a painful process, I decided.

It was within the next two days that the ultimate in journeys was embarked upon. The call of the Isles was a potent influence, emphasised in the many brochures and pamphlets now being studied by the grown-ups. I scarcely dared hope that this call would reach the stage of realisation.

To my infinite satisfaction, a rail-trip to Kyle of Lochalsh was, however, decided upon and it was with great excitement that we boarded the Kyle train at Inverness station and crept engine-forward round the leg of the triangle over which we had entered 'backwards' on our arrival at Inverness, less than a week before. Yet, by virtue of our 'action-packed' explorations of the town and surrounding county, that arrival now seemed quite remote.

As I recall it, the seating obtained on the train was at a window-side table in an 'open third' coach (which were not widely utilised at that time other than on trains of a tourist nature). All of us were intensely interested in the landscape through which we travelled and I believe that it was a fact that only one of the group had been any further than a few miles beyond Inverness. My uncle had been an avid and compulsive reader from childhood and my father had read, also, quite widely and had a broad general knowledge. Many aspects of the history and geography of the terrain to be traversed were anticipated and discussed with some animation, as we travelled along.

The crossing of the Ness was an almost immediate source of interest, with rapid attempts to identify our well-trod river-bank walks down-river. Then there came Clachnaharry cabin, close to the starting point of our recent canal adventure. Beyond there came long glimpses of the Beauly Firth – that extension of the parent Moray Firth. Many years were to elapse before a bridge would render the Kessock ferry redundant and open up a fast road to the ultimate north and present a formidable challenge to the capital-starved railway of the future.

Beauly and Muir of Ord (with its branching tentacle to

Fortrose in the Black Isle) constituted unknown territory and were scrutinised accordingly. Then came Dingwall with its junction from the line to Wick and Thurso and exhilaration from the belief that at last we were truly headed for the Isles. Immediately thereafter, a branch seemed to be discerned heading downhill to the left, but it was some years later that reading identified this as the erstwhile branch to Strathpeffer, which in Highland Railway days had boasted six branch trains in either direction to the graceful terminus of that Victorian 'spa'.

Across the Moors; through Plockton and within sight of the Cuchullins

The moorland that followed, by my personally synthesised definition, had, I reckoned, a true Highland aspect and the place and station names had an authentic ring. Could one better a selection than Auchterneed, Lochluichart, Achanalt, Achnasheen and Achnashellach? There was joy in the heart; but further excitement was to come!

To my astonishment (or perhaps consternation is the more accurate term) a decision was taken that we should have a meal in the dining car and thither we shortly made our way. This was certainly a 'first off' and it met my fullest expectations. I feel certain that we did not rise to the maximum tariff level; but whatever we had was excellent.

That was the first of many restaurant-car meals, the vast majority on company business; but, in retrospect, how excellent were these traditional meals. The mind returns to contemplation of such peripherals as kippers, toast and marmalade, and so much else that was excellent. What more civilised joy could one wish than to be served in comfort with delicious fare, while the pleasing countryside rolls past and interesting conversation flourishes.

The finest service we ever received was during my honeymoon, fifteen years later, on the way from Waterloo to Bournemouth, when we ordered a 'simple' breakfast which (when the steward learned we were from Fife) miraculously extended to non-stop provision from platform end to platform end. Perhaps that is the meaning of the term 'banquet' and it persuaded me (if such persuasion was necessary) that nothing can excel rail travel – but, of course, it is not given to all mankind to be born Fifers ...

As we neared Strome Ferry, we gazed with awe on the extent of the deep rock cuttings and the massive civil-engineering features of that section of line, generally. The expense of such construction was reckoned as awesome in the extreme.

My uncle fell into conversation with an off-duty railway man bound for Skye and came back well-furnished with details of the line and the communities who depended on it.

Plockton was passed and its natural beauties extolled. Thither I would one day return to absorb its glories at close range and I feel sure its charm could never pall. Soon eyes were turned to the north-west as we eagerly sought to catch a glimpse of the far Cuchullins between the rocky environs.

In a short time we were through Duirinish and the rock gouges before the terminus to draw slowly to a stand at Kyle of Lochalsh platform.

To Kyleakin by boat in sight of Castle Maol; Stornoway boats; more civil works *en route*; Skyemen v Napoleon and sundry other irrelevant musings

We climbed down and made our way up the busy platform, with the Isle of Skye appearing from beyond a hidden channel to loom up apparently just beyond the buffers. I again marvelled at this amazing amalgam of a busy terminus set cheek by jowl with all the beauties of the wildest country imaginable.

Having penetrated so far to the west, it was decided that it was imperative that a visit should be paid to Skye and so the small ferry was boarded and we all crossed to Kyleakin. In the process we scrutinised all the features of the kyle – or narrows – between the island and the mainland, including Castle Maol, which could be seen on the island shore, to the left of Kyleakin.

From the landing stage we pressed on to the periphery of the village. Time, however was short and there was no latitude, as to be left behind in Kyle would have raised major problems – not the least of them financial. In spite of this, it was decided to walk towards Broadford and off we set with the channel on our right, roughly parallel to the road which we were following. In a short time, a large Macbrayne vessel sailed into sight and headed north. This, we subsequently discovered, was the afternoon boat to Stornoway. Such sailings have long since disappeared, as the rail to ship facilities of many years were abandoned in favour of road connections through Ullapool, thus rendering the viability of Kyle of Lochalsh (and its rail-link) highly fragile.

It would seem that over the years there has been a concerted, co-ordinated and highly effective plan to destroy the railway system and all the facilities built up so remarkably by the past and more foreseeing generations. It never ceased to nauseate across the years, when politicians proclaimed their love for railways as a system of transport and described their unstinting efforts in securing the well-being of rail, when it seemed chillingly apparent that the inevitable consequences of so much of their subsequent legislation must have entailed the ultimate demise of the network.

No such diabolic machinations had been set afoot on that clear and sunny July afternoon and such thoughts did not enter the minds of the party. One sombre issue was discussed however. My father referred to the vast number of Skye men who had joined the British Army to fight Napoleon. Against this total the present island population seemed to illustrate the huge reductions effected by the Highland Clearances. My uncle made reference to Boswell's account of Dr Johnson's visit to Skye. Possibly Raasay was mentioned as it would have been visible from our vantage point (especially Dun Can where the ebullient Boswell danced his jig) but memory fails me on such detail.

It became obvious that some work was proceeding on our road and in a short time we came across a bridge under construction.

With the limited equipment of that time (by comparison with today's cornucopia of mechanical wonders) the project appeared a formidable one. Construction workers were in evidence, both at roadway level and in the minor ravine.

There was some interchange with one man, I recall – perhaps he merely asked the time. I thought of my fellow traveller of some days ago and wondered how he had fared in a search for work and continuity. I surveyed the *glaur* which was everywhere, the streamlets and other waters oozing from the moorland and bog. I imagined the winds whistling from the channel and the temperature on winter mornings. I thought of the isolation one might feel and the possibly primitive eating and sleeping conditions and the more rudimentary task of keeping clean. There was, I imagined, the possible problem of compatibility with one's mates.

'Must be a hard life,' I concluded – but there lay a challenge.

Easier, meantime, to think of the scenic wonders all around; or even of Castle Maol and its legendary use as a toll bar to shipping by a Norse Amazon. One would need to be a strong, wild man or woman to operate that ploy! Enlistment to fight Napoleon did not seem a bed of roses, either. A host of Macleods had experienced that call and had not grumbled. A great reward some from Sutherland received when they suffered eviction and had their cottages burned down! One of my forebears had fought in the Peninsula and returned to Caledonia, it was said. Another (on the Munro side) had been through the winter at Balaclava and seen the Heights of Alma scaled, whilst yet another on that side had been to India, in a surrounded, outback fort!

Meantime, it was easier to contemplate the way back to the station! But first: how far away was Broadford? Too far! so it was some twenty-five years later when I reached there and life, by then, was 'not so bad' – though like many another, I still grumbled. But perhaps that was but one aspect of life and life is sweet whatever the obstacle. '*Nil desperandum carborundum,*' the 'shop' philosophers had it. There is some comfort in that ambivalent stance.

Yet there are higher challenges and a greater reward. 'He who tholes survives,' proclaimed the slogan on the ancient gable by the Royal Mile, Chambers tells us in his memoirs, and so has reasoned many a dogged Scot. What thoughts might have had the Norse King Haakon as he sailed through the Kyle on his way to Largs and defeat?

Sufficient musings for the moment! So to our tale!

Farewell to the Kyle: a railyard in the wilds

With longing glances towards the Kyle – a serene prospect on that sunny afternoon, with blue sky above and not a hint of the rain-saturated gloom which can settle over the island (as certain visits, many years later, were to demonstrate) – we made an 'about turn' and reluctantly made our way back to the diminutive ferry. To set foot on Skye had been a bonus and the severely limited time available to us had been a pre-condition. Yet if our miniscule penetration of the island had defied reason, it had but been supplanted by a wilder desire to explore the greater unknown lands to the north and, indeed, the whole island.

Back to the train we went, and a rapid overview of the station scene was (to me, at least) some small compensation for our truncated exploration. It seemed quite remarkable that scope for so much activity could have been won from that rocky shore; and to witness trains marshalled and routine station activities carried on in that unlikely site seemed quite remarkable.

Soon after boarding, the train drew out and we settled down to capture any elements of the landscape which might have been missed on our outward journey, and to extract the full essence of the route's compelling beauty. One benefit of our close scrutiny was an excellent glimpse of a herd of deer beyond Achnasheen.

The consensus was that it had been an excellent day's outing and the spell of the West Highlands had been laid or intensified on all members of the party. For me, the prospect of our return rail-journey home was the only counterbalance to the rapidly growing gloom that came with the journey's end and the accentuated realisation that the holiday was very close to its end.

CHAPTER 18

In 1939, on the last family holiday, we make a rail journey to Stirling; a hiker is sighted

One more major holiday with my family (parents, brother, aunt and uncle) was to afford the opportunity for a new rail-travel experience and – occurring in July 1939 – it was to be the last of its kind.

The selected venue was Callander and, as before, the time was the Kirkcaldy Trades holiday week.

Once again, the Saturday morning of that week saw the group waiting at Kirkcaldy Station but, on this occasion, on the southbound platform. As before and to my delight, many trains (not a few of which were specials) passed through the station, and their locomotives were scrutinised with great interest. One northbound locomotive arrested attention, being of a totally unknown class and exhibiting a rather unusual feature. This was later identified as an LNER B12 class locomotive and the unaccustomed feature defined as a feed-heating apparatus, the most prominent elements of which were two large cylinders mounted pannier-fashion on the boiler barrel crown and fed by prominent pipework.

In Fife Sheds, I believe these engines were nicknamed 'Hikers' because of these pannier-like cylinders; but this may cause confusion as certain engines were so called for an entirely different reason: the considerable distance between tender and backplate. On the GNSR section, to which some of these engines were allocated for their light axle loading, they were nicknamed Hikers because of the distance traversed by the fireman betwixt tender and firebox door. The pre-heating system was of the ACFI type and fitted experimentally. I believe Dabeg, Weir and Worthington systems were also experimented with around that period and my recollection may require checking.

There were many of the old familiar classes in evidence that morning (with ex-NBR engines prominent, as always in 'our' sector).

Once again, our little band was fortunate, as a direct train had been provided for Stirling passengers via Dunfermline and Alloa. This also held great interest as much of that route was still completely unknown to me.

The first portion of the route – to Aberdour – was that taken by all Edinburgh trains and so by reasonably familiar track. We did not, of course, enter Inverkeithing but utilised the 'east' leg of the triangular junctions which afforded direct-running to Burntisland for freight and coal traffic from the Alloa line and that portion of the West Fife coalfield comprising Cowdenbeath, Kelty and Lochgelly (Burntisland being still a significant coal-exporting port). This proved to be the first (and, alas, the last) occasion on which I was to travel over that connecting spur.

Dunfermline was, by 1939, reasonably well known territory but the section from there to Stirling via Alloa was completely unknown and therefore extremely interesting. That journey is very fresh in the memory: in fact, almost as if it had occurred yesterday. It is strange how minor episodes lurk in the memory and assist in defining certain occasions.

As we approached Dunfermline Lower, my father happened to be glancing through the local paper which he had possibly stuffed into his pocket as we left home, Saturday being the day of delivery. This contained news of the appointment of a new head of 'science' for Kirkcaldy High School: a Dr Guthrie who was to remove from St Andrews where he had been assistant Head of Science. This was indeed news to me but he was to be one of my teachers for some years to come. It seems unbelievable that several years have elapsed since his death (which occurred after many years of service in education) and yet the recall of that small incident has the clarity of a statement from last week.

Leaving the western extremity of the Fife coalfield, it was not long before the Hillfoots region, below the Ochil range, could be espied away to our right and after Alloa (whose size and railway ramifications surprised me) the branch lines to Menstrie and Alva were noted and the western extremity of the Ochils scrutinised. My aunt was much interested in this area as she had spent memorable holidays with a college friend in Blairlogie and had found that village and its wider environs most appealing. The Carse of Stirling was now in evidence and, not long thereafter, Causewayhead; the Wallace Monument provided a fruitful source of discussion. By then, Stirling was obviously close at hand and very shortly we were curving towards the station approaches.

Though not in my 'grand' category, as Perth undoubtedly had seemed, the extent and traffic of Stirling I found impressive and this was intensified by the fact that it was totally unknown to me and, obviously, another stronghold of the LMS, being on their main-line from London and Glasgow to Aberdeen.

Not long after detraining we found the Callander train. For a very short time, we appeared to be retracing our tracks but the geography of Stirling and its railways soon became apparent and we identified the line from Fife curving away toward the Ochils, after first hugging the hill whose summit was crowned by the towering monument to Scotland's soldier and patriot, Sir William Wallace.

'Our' line, on the other hand, was heading for the gap between the terminal slopes of the Ochils and a hill-mass to the West.

Callander and Trossachs bound

The country through which we passed, on our way to Bridge of Allan, seemed to hold great promise, I thought; but on this holiday I had no major preconceptions other than a belief that the Trossachs should be romantically beautiful. Sir Walter Scott's

'Lady of the Lake' had been set there. This work (after 'Marmion') had been one of the early works read in the English class before moving on to *The Merchant of Venice*. The work had seemed interesting as there had been a story to follow and anything Scottish had had additional attraction. The fact that 'James Fitzjames' and 'Ellen Douglas' were well regarded engines also helped.

A more potent attraction, possibly, was that sectors of the region featured in some of my uncle's yarns of excursions and tramps into the wilds. His tales had a strong appeal for me as they inevitably related to terrain and modes of life unknown and hence induced an undefined aura of mystery and excitement and invoked potential exploration to see for oneself. Names such as Loch Katrine, Sronachlachar and the Duke's Pass induced such an aura and were inherently attractive.

Wider peripherals such as Glen Dochart, Glen Falloch and Strathyre seemed to imply a call to tramp. 'Where twines the path' seemed to have the professional pull of the poet! Immediately envisaged were sun-dappled paths through labyrinthine forests with hidden glades and perhaps a leaping burn or dark lochan unfolding as they wound. Now, I was coming to find out – and such could scarcely fail to be interesting!

At Dunblane the church was noted beside the fast flowing Allan Water but likewise the junction with the main line curving away in cutting to climb for Perth some great distance away! Thereafter, it was apparent that we were on a secondary line. Could this be so? More to investigate in the week ahead!

To the left a sizeable river appeared, more visible after Doune. In a short time crags were seen to rise on the left and the arrival at Callander cut out further speculation.

The station was a surprise: in spite of its size, timber was included in construction. One accepted Thornton because of those woes arising from subterranean extraction, but to have a 'big' station made with some wooden features seemed odd. How this weird impression arose, I now know not. Strange mixture this LMS organisation! But the town looked desirable and the adjacent houses grand and of noble proportions.

'Hope that the residence selected is not some log-cabin,' I mused. But on we marched to announce our arrival and so we should soon know the worst!

A riverbank knoll; Black Fives (?) in tandem

The boarding house which was to be our base for the next week was situated in the Main Street and was a douce, solid and well-maintained establishment, as befitted its environs, neighbouring structures and the town generally.

It was not far from an important bridge over the Teith and somewhere behind it lay a pleasant water-meadow close to the water's edge, from which rose a small knoll or mound with a Gaelic name. Adjacent to this, a far-seeing authority had provided a number of comfortable seats, strategically placed, for appreciation of the calm and pleasing riverside view. As ever, many were the walks and explorations made to evaluate the town's environs and capture the charms of the noted beauty spots, by river, hill and wood.

Around meal times, however, it became a practice, as weather permitted, to forgather in that spot to discuss the wonders seen, rest weary limbs on occasion and, perhaps, discuss the strategy for the hours or days ahead. Other groups would do likewise, and in pauses in our conversation, snatches of their talk would be wafted across and mostly ignored. Such times of intermission in some instances arose from study of the daily paper or, quite frequently, from the perusal of pamphlets or guide books relating to the district. One small group was obviously from the 'Lang Toun' as I deduced, with some difficulty, from an interchange between my father and uncle conducted *sotto voce*. It is strange how such minor irrelevances are pinned in memory to the scenes in which they were experienced. Such was the case in this instance:

The 'overheard one' spoke loudly, without trace of any Fife accent or Doric usage, and with a positive, assertive manner, as one in authority. I must admit that I felt compelled to eavesdrop as the subject appeared to be an assessment of favourite or famous comedians and names were wafted on the breeze, of which, in days ahead, I might be knowledgeable, but which, when heard, conveyed nothing. A seemingly regular performer to 'Fifer' audiences was spoken of with veneration and nostalgia: Charlie Kemble by name. Many, many years later when I read his obituary my thoughts returned to that grassy river-bank. The man with the name related to the patois or patter of Kelvinside, I never saw, nor do I know the identity of his admirer, but, as a mordant fixes dye, so Charles Campbell fixed one aspect of immediately pre-Second World War Callander.

Rambles there were a-plenty in the area. Happy wanderings by the banks of Teith and Lenny are vividly recalled, as are treks to nearby Kilmahog (with its water-wheel-driven woollen-mill. Likewise an evening climb to the Bracklinn Falls and the return in the borrowed light from the western glories of a setting sun. There were also walks toward Loch Lubnaig and on the lower shoulder of Ben Ledi to view Samson's Putting Stone. The two latter routes were a particular lure for me as they closely approached the railway in their early stages and, indeed, provided desirable vantage points, from which to view 'double-headers' (Black Fives) snaking in either direction with their long passenger trains.

Non-rail excursions to Loch Katrine's *Sir Walter Scott*

Exploration was not confined to pedestrian activities alone. Several excursions were successfully made on bus tours organised by a local company. Mostly short trips these were, and it became a feature of these runs that several faces tended to re-appear amongst the passengers. My brother at that time was quite young, around nine years of age.

Two of the recurrent faces which became familiar were those

of a young couple, who if not a honeymoon couple appeared to be approaching that stage. They were brimming with life and enthusiasm. They seemed to attract my brother and, on tour, they would summon him to the rear seat and there was constant hilarity from that quarter in which he would join. Donald and Belle, they were. Not only did their giggles and their patter enliven the journeys, but so full of life and joy were they that they inevitably burst into song. One 'hit' of the day was 'Down Mexico Way', and regardless of the terrain or passing scene, the strains of that song rang through the bus. Their happiness and zest seemed to strike a chord with even the older more staid passengers and broke down any pockets of potential gloom. Ships that pass in the night is, I suppose, the usual cliché; but I have often wondered how life subsequently dealt with them. War was declared within two months. Was Donald called to the forces? Did he survive the war? Idle speculation, for we shall never know; but such is mankind's inherent curiosity.

One tour took us to Loch Katrine, where we walked by the lochside. We also saw at the pier that remarkable steamship that is now a veteran but steaming on, albeit with a new boiler recently fitted.

Many were the other venues, but Loch Vennacher, Brig o' Turk and Falls of Lenny are but some recalled.

Chapter 19

Gareloch's depression metaphor; Wee Davy and the Philipstines and a Scottish Gaucho

The most unusual excursion by road occurred one afternoon, when it was decided that we should, again, sample one of the local bus tours – that which scheduled Loch Lomond and the Lake of Menteith amongst its venues. Presumably from the popularity of this particular itinerary and a degree of procrastination in the group's decision, we turned up some minutes late to find that the bus was fully booked. To our considerable surprise, we were offered, as an alternative, a car with driver, which we accepted with alacrity.

Our route followed the now-familiar road by Kilmahog and Loch Lubnaig and thence by Strathyre and Lochearnhead to Glen Dochart and Crianlarich. Unfortunately the afternoon was sunless, with leaden skies, but this did not dampen our enthusiasm nor diminish our eager scrutiny of the encountered landscape.

Heading down to Crianlarich, scanning the peaks for the location of Ben Dorain, I knew that we must be coming into West Highland Line territory, as indeed we were. Thus, shortly we passed under the bridge, carrying the then little-used spur which connected the LMS and LNER lines and which is now a part of the only remaining railway connection between Glasgow and Oban. From Crianlarich we ran through Glen Falloch and stopped to examine the Falls of Falloch in their gorge setting whose walls, it seemed, were ominously undercut by the intensity of the hastening River Falloch on its downward course. At Tarbet, my father mentioned the Viking invaders who, it seemed, had dragged their vessels overland from Loch Long to gain access to Loch Lomond. We were to follow their route.

Later, as we crossed a ridge and descended to the Gareloch, we were confronted by a panoramic view of a great armada of laid-up ships anchored in the loch below. Those vessels had been laid up, some, possibly, for a considerable time as palpable victims of the Great Depression, only now showing real evidence of termination, but about to be massively accelerated by the stimulus of war. Some were awaiting the breakers' yard.

My eye was drawn to one vessel of unusual design and eye-catching cut which remained in my memory for a considerable time. For long, I had hopes that some reference would be encountered that would bring identification. The hopefully definitive nature of her two bulky funnels, set transversely to the ship's longitudinal centre line, was one cardinal characteristic, as also was her apparently unusually broad beam. No clue to her identity have I so far found. The party surveyed the host of ships with considerable interest, but without binoculars, identification of the individual craft was severely limited.

The onward road from that vantage point was by Helensburgh, and there I had my first view of the Clyde Estuary of which I had heard so much from family sources, not least my father and my uncle. We did not dally by the estuarine regions, however, but pressed on upwards and climbed a road by pleasantly-situated, garden-girdled villas, well endowed with sweepingly magnificent estuarine vistas. From these halcyon heights we descended once more (through Glen Fruin to Loch Lomond-side) and entered a more mundane region on the fringe of Balloch.

Shortly, Balloch Park was pointed out on the further shore of the loch. This must have been the site of one of my earliest memories, which only now has lost the vivid clarity of a few years back. Though of a gossamer and highly vulnerable consistency, my recollection is of standing towards the rear of a group of unfamiliar children, slightly greater in years perhaps, on a green and grassy incline running down to a water's edge and fringed by lofty trees. A man was relating a story to the group and holding their wrapt attention.

The tale was of 'Wee Davy and the Philipstines' (an actual text version of which I only encountered a few months ago in an anthology of Scottish writing). When I endeavoured to obtain an explanation and date for this recalled event from my mother, she was able to fill in the detail and give the identity of the story-teller as a Mr John Richmond, whom I recalled as having met one Sunday evening, when walking with my grandfather some years after that event and whose son was the foreman under whom my father had worked for several years. This incident must have occurred when I was possibly three and a half years old, around early summer 1929.

From Balloch, the homeward route was by Drymen, Aberfoyle and Port of Menteith. On the way, there was mention of Glasgow's water supply and the pipes of formidable diameter forming a portion of the aqueduct were encountered. There was talk of Robert Bontine Cunningham Graham, so much associated with this area, an erstwhile politician, patriot and *gaucho* from the Pampas, whose written words only came into my possession a few years ago. He seemed, from their comments on that day, to be a hero of both my father and my uncle. There was also reference to a more legendary hero of the region: Rob Roy Macgregor, and to his exploits and depredations.

All of these snippets from a continuing broad discussion remain lucidly in the memory, as are the references which were made to Flanders Moss and to Lake Menteith – the only Scottish lake.

I found it tantalising that we had been so close to the Clydeside region, of which I had heard so much and of which I would dearly have loved a glimpse, but to extend our visit thence would have been patently ridiculous.

By this time the sun had returned and lit up the braes as we wound our way over the ridge, beyond which lurked 'the varied realms of fair Menteith' and the town of Callander. Soon after the descent, we drew over the bridge adjacent to our favoured water meadow rendezvous and, turning left, the car deposited us at the boarding house which was to remain our quarters for but a few more days.

On the Callander and Oban line we view the Lenny viaduct and Glen Ogle; we sense awe in the pass of Brander and catch a first glimpse of Oban Bay

Two unforgettable expeditions were made by rail.

To my intense satisfaction, a decision was taken to visit Oban, and we set off around ten o'clock on the selected morning from Callander Station, along with a number of like-minded travellers, on a train from Stirling. As in the case of the previous year's Kyle of Lochalsh expedition, we travelled in an 'open-third', and were fortunate in having a table to ourselves. This provided an excellent vantage point from which to scan the rewarding scenery of that fine route. The train was double headed, as was commonplace on that route. I am tempted to suggest two 'Black Fives' as our motive power, but I took no

22. The Callander and Oban Railway beside the river Lenny. (Hartmann Postcard)

notes and memory is not now to be trusted on that particular point. It is scant compensation for such a fundamental omission but I do claim to recall their deep-throated blast later in the journey, as they drew their heavy train up Glen Ogle, past the Pulpit Rock.

Loch Lubnaig was intently scrutinised from this new rail-angle, and the impressive bow-string-girder bridge over the Falls of Lenny admired. Strathyre was scanned with a great

23. The Killin branch in British Railways days: tank engine of Caledonian Railway, McIntosh design. Tractive effort 18,679 lb. Built at St Rollox, 1914. (Photo: Author, early 50s)

expectancy (partially inspired by the well-familiar Scots song) as were the Braes of Balquidder beyond. In the Glen Ogle approaches, Lochearnhead lay far below and the connection from Perth could be traced by the eye as it receded back along the loch-side. Balquidder station was the junction for this line; and its ramifications seemed somewhat grand in this lonely and comparatively remote spot amidst the hills. The climb up Glen Ogle was a rare experience and it was a tragedy when this section of railway was lost forever by the untimely land-slip that clinched the planned closure. As I recall, the railway authority later had a dramatic poster which captured the compelling beauty of that most impressive climb up and along that seemingly precarious ledge gouged and bracketed from the mountainside.

The little junction for Killin was viewed with some surprise (but it was to be in post-war days that I sampled the joys of the little branch train behind its Caley Tank gliding down the formidable bank to the tiny station, beyond which lay the Loch Tay pier, which I was never to have the opportunity to explore. From Killin Junction the line ran down through Glen Dochart – explored on our previous safari by road – and so to Crianlarich (where I hoped that there just might have been the opportunity of seeing a West Highland Train as the two lines crossed (and were spur-connected) at that village, as demonstrated by our earlier exploration. The elevated interconnector was consequently scrutinised with expectant intensity. Between Crianlarich and Tyndrum, I continued to scan the moorland terrain for traces of the West Highland line whose track could just be seen running along the hillside opposite but was not fortunate enough to see any trace of a West Highland train.

On we went, through new territory, by Glen Orchy and Dalmally, where we were able to attach well known names to new and so far unknown places. Surrounded by the fine scenery around the southern end of Loch Awe lay Kilchurch Castle. This region was much admired but the location that inspired most and fed the imagination was that around the awesome upper narrows of the loch in the Pass of Brander. I sought to imagine the difficulties and hazards which must have faced the constructors of the line and immensely admired their efforts. The eerieness of the scene as I recall it, then, is not recaptured nowadays. Then the pass seemed much narrower and the dark, ominous water somehow more sinister.

The road has now, of course, been driven through the narrows

– a task by no means undeserving of praise, but indubitably tackled with more sophisticated plant and equipment than that available to the railway construction team. Some time ago I was able to speak to one of the roadway contractors, who described the task as just another difficult contract – a serious understatement I would aver.

At that point in the journey, the line was passing along the base of Ben Cruachan (from whose rocky interior a vast cavernous power station has since been excavated) and a series of curious double-armed signals were espied. These excited the curiosity and it was some years later that I learned their actual function: as a warning device to alert drivers to the presence of stray boulders which were prone to rattle down the mountainside and onto the track. The twin arms were actuated by trip-wires parallel to the track but at an appropriate distance up the mountainside. On being contacted by a boulder these would bring the twin (opposed) arms into the horizontal (danger) position and thus give warning to the driver.

After Taynuilt, Loch Etive became the focus of interest and at its western end the Falls of Lora. The major source of interest was then the fine cantilever bridge at Connell Ferry, carrying the branch railway to Ballachulish beside Loch Leven.

From that point, it did not seem long till we were passing Glen Cruitten and then running down the final gradient to catch our first glimpse of Oban Bay and fall smitten by its magic – in a spell that would beckon for many a year.

Bonny Strathyre by train and an ultimate and reluctant departure from the Trossachs; post war circular rail-tours; the magic carpet of rail that has gone forever

A short train journey was to provide the last excursion before departure and had as its destination Kingshouse platform, which was the next station down the line from Strathyre, and a short distance beyond. This short journey was a repetition in part, therefore, of our Oban experience.

The day was one of sunshine and the Braes of Strathyre and Balquidder seemed full of promise, while the hills to the west seemed to call for exploration. The desired, ultimate destination was Rob Roy's grave in the tiny churchyard of Balquidder, and Loch Voil, beyond that point, positively sparkled in the late morning sunshine.

It was quite impressive to have such a 'grand' train stop for us at our wayside platform, but such was the broad potential for country-wide exploration in that happy age of the train when the railway gave access to virtually every nook and cranny of the countryside. It is an exquisite form of torture to sit down with a timetable of the twenties or to a lesser extent that of the forties and to enumerate the host of fascinating train-based rambles which one could have joyfully completed from points that were, effectively, on one's own doorstep (i.e. from a small Lowland village).

Father and uncle were both well versed in Scott and in the manifold legends of Rob Roy Macgregor; their enthusiasm spilled over and we all walked with a will. The churchyard and the burial spot were readily found and the rustic beauty of the adjacent scene, with a boisterous streamlet cascading beneath its rustic bridge, absorbed the group and was, in turn, ecstatically admired.

On our return we held southward to terminate at Strathyre station, where we paused on its wide platform whilst awaiting our train for Callander. From that vantage point we scrutinised every particle of the adjacent scenery in a communal uncertainty as to when we should pass that way again.

Saturday morning came all too soon after that excursion and when it dawned, it was one of lowering skies and very heavy rain. The south-bound platform was packed, and until the train arrived, the crowd sought shelter under the adequate canopies. On its arrival the travellers eagerly sought the positive shelter and comforting warmth of individual compartments, from which, as we headed for Doune, I eagerly scanned for a final glance at the River Teith, on whose banks we had so often strolled, or rested while the yarns went round.

In later years I was to pass a number of times through Callander, *en route* for Oban; but the most of these outward journeys were to be made in the hours of dusk.

At the station, I only once again de-trained, around 1953 when, bound on a rail-tour that incorporated a bus journey (the modern equivalent of the horse drawn vehicle of the early years) by Loch Katrine Stronachlachar and the bumpy descent to Inversnaid to embark on PS *King Edward* for Balloch and thence by train to dear old Glasgow. Yet, such delights were all but fading, even then; and 1955 *et sequitur* 'saw to all' such manifestations of 'financial nonsense'.

For me, however, subsequent visits to Callander, pleasantly rewarding as they were, could never repeat the magic of 1939. (But, in wider contemplation, how many other spells were broken in the fateful years, which followed?)

As I was so repeatedly to experience, the realisation dawned that it is a unique amalgam of place and people which creates such moments of magic. The personalities involved, with all their enthusiasms, knowledge, views and experience, together with the friendships forged and the relationships reinforced, are the catalyst which releases that magic. The locus, no matter how divinely beautiful, cannot in itself re-create these charismatic moments; nor should we expect it to so do.

Chapter 20

Railway men in retrospect: their character, wit and response to the daily demands of their job; the war pressures on the rail system

To recall these early journeys and evoke the spirit of the railway system as it was then, one must also recapture the character of those who were involved as operators and even passengers, something which no archival photograph painting or reconstruction can ever reproduce, no matter how expert, admirable and professional the quality of these artefacts may be.

How exquisite were these railway experiences – not only the sights, the sounds and no less the 'feel' of these railway journeys, but above all the character of the railway men, observed in their wit and in their actions as they reacted or responded to the tasks (often severe) imposed upon them by the weather; the state of the equipment; the schedules; the omniscient rule book; the nature of the fuel; the exigencies arising and the whims of the travelling public or the variations in the merchandise conveyed; not to mention the hours demanded by mandate or by fickle circumstance; and the remuneration provided. Only an experience and cognisance of such diverse factors – many targeted by the 'slings and arrows of outrageous fortune' – in that particularly demanding period in time, can capture the authentic railway experience.

Perhaps the perceived magic was in the locomotive and the implied skill of the designer and the artificer, to which it was witness. Yet without the crew the locomotive was worthless and it indubitably was the combination of man and machine (with the input of all other supportive grades) that produced the spectacle and created these transport experiences that are of such a calibre as to be unforgettable.

Perhaps the urgency and vibrancy conveyed by many of these memories stems from the role which the railways then played as an essential supporter of the national life. Perhaps, in part, it may stem from the overall atmosphere pervading a nation at war, when everywhere there was essential action and movement and a universal sense of urgency and realism.

'Have No Truck With Delay' proclaimed the goods depot poster.

Was Your Journey essential? did not other posters – festooning every station – demand!

Servicemen were returning to duty; others returned on a highly-constricted period of leave. War-workers were travelling to or from work. Some were moving to far-off new workplaces.

In stations, especially large units such as Waverley, one could sense the urgency of it all, even the pathos and the apprehension that seemed to pervade sectors of the scene. Service-men hastened from and to the RTO offices which had sprung up, while others crowded around the exterior in small apprehensive groups. Crowds would descend from crammed long-distance trains ('over twenty bogies behind the tender' being almost a commonplace rather than a miracle).

Others, many laden with kit, would push aboard into jammed corridors. The sorrows of charged partings or the joys of reunion would be enacted in little groups seeking impossible privacy.

Elsewhere routine travellers would entrain in their regular rake of carriages, if in blackout hours, furnished with minimal illumination. Barrows of mail or parcels would be avoided by the rushing throng. Whistles would shrill! Engines emerging from the Calton tunnel and making for No. 19 platform would give their final echoing blasts before depositing their coaches. Everywhere there would be action and everywhere movement!

And for the enthusiasts and cognoscenti there would be engines and action aplenty across the station's wide domains.

CHAPTER 21

Coruscations: to the North with two 'eighteen-inchers'

For me, a favourite observation point for the passing locomotive scene was a footpath which hugged the northbound railway from Dysart station for a substantial distance before joining a main roadway (Randolph Road). As well as allowing close proximity to the main line, this gave a vantage point for observation of the mineral branch to the Frances Colliery (known locally as the Dubby) and its adjacent yard, where the outgoing coal trains were marshalled. Much shunting was involved at this point and it was inevitable that one locomotive would be in attendance here (in the majority of cases of J37 class although J35, J36 and J38 classes would, no doubt, be seen from time to time).

Many were the walks and rambles contrived to incorporate that pathway as the starting or even finishing section of the route.

It is, perhaps, not surprising therefore that one of my most unique recollections took place on that favoured section of footpath. The date was around the autumn of 1943 and therefore in wartime; and, as the hour was around 9.00 p.m., the evening darkness was falling. As my father and I progressed northward, there was no initial sign of activity. Shortly, however, we became aware of an approaching train, at some distance to the south, the location defined by the din in that quarter and confirmed very shortly by a vision of a sky that was backcloth to a mass of violently upward-shooting embers. We anticipated that an exceptionally heavy freight train would at any moment draw into sight.

The fading light of that autumn evening now served as a pale background to twin columns of sparks, shooting violently skyward and tinged at their peripheries with contrasting dark smoke and fleecy steam. These conjoined terminally in a maelstrom of sparks and embers. The rasping and barking continued to imply a massive application of tractive effort somewhere up the line, the locus of which was growing closer by the minute, as defined by the approaching high-level coruscations. We were compelled to stop as we eagerly awaited a close-range examination of this phenomenon, which was rending the normal, relaxed Saturday evening calm of this semi-rural fringe.

Gradually the indistinct profile of two locomotives was thrust into sight. Behind them there were drawn not a long chain of freight or mineral wagons as these displays of sound and light conjured in the mind; but instead our astonished gaze focused on a lengthy string of mainline coaches whose tail was now snaking past Dysart signal box.

Onward strained the toiling pair beneath a living mass of steam and shooting embers. The generated din was earsplitting; but they were making ever-increasing headway, as they accelerated their formidable load on the flank of the continuous rise to the summit, lying in darkness in the cutting to the north-east by Randolph Colliery Signal Box.

This was, certainly, a moment to be recalled: two J36s hauling the Aberdeen express, and making a lusty and demanding effort to hold time, no doubt after some engine failure to the south.

Such were the unsung victories of a railway at war: meeting a nigh impossible challenge head-on, whenever it came, and above all the stringent and random demand of such exigencies: keeping the wheels moving and the traffic flowing in those arteries of the nation's body corporate.

Chapter 22

A revelation in locomotive classification; the morning workman's train; blowers give a practical lesson in resonance

For some twenty years (from approximately 1942 till 1962) the railway system impinged significantly on my life, in the sense that for substantial periods during that time span I was an intensive user of its facilities and was thus able to observe railway operation in a period of change and challenge.

My early interest in railway matters was thus given renewal and intensification as I regularly observed both the equipment and the workforce in performance of their duties, meeting the challenges which fate had in store for them during that crucial period.

I was never a 'train-spotter' in the true definition of that term, nor might I have been accurately termed a 'student of railways' in any academic sense. In many ways my observations ran parallel to that of both such observers but possibly lacked the fanaticism of the former and the total dedication of the latter. For me the railway scene inspired a deep empathy and by a strange twist of fate I was offered and gladly accepted the opportunity to study locomotive engineering as a branch of mechanical engineering, which in turn (by a combination of fate, enthusiasm and positive reasoning) I had selected as my desired sphere of activity and profession in life.

As a child, becoming more aware of the railway presence in my environment, I, like many others, started to jot down engine numbers, but in those days I had no concept of locomotive classification nor any rational notion of their relative capabilities or, indeed, origins. Regular observation gradually promoted the thought that behind the numbers lay some reasoned system, if for no other reason than the fact that the 'older' LNER locomotives (all from the former NBR stud – as I learned later) seemed to carry numbers starting with 9000. Further pause for thought was induced by the observation that numbers starting with 6000 were allocated to the 'Director' class (as I much later learned to call them) as well as the small shunting 'tankies' with the stovepipe chimneys and unaccustomed forward dome locations, which shunted intensively at Kirkcaldy and Sinclairtown goods-yards as 'pilots'.

A sudden revelation came in 1938 whilst on holiday in Tayport with my aunt. It was decided, one day, that my aunt would take my brother and me to Montrose for the afternoon. This, naturally, demanded a rail journey – entailing a change of trains at Dundee Taybridge Station.

Whilst waiting there for the northbound express, I espied on the bookstall a slim paper-covered booklet entitled (I think) *Locomotives of the LNER* and published by the Locomotive Publishing Co. Ltd., London and advertised by the *Railway Magazine*, whose cost precluded me from the regular readership of that journal. At that moment, however, I was sufficiently solvent to procure the coveted document and carry it off with joy. From the moment of opening its covers, the whole concept of locomotive classification became apparent. No doubt serious analytical study should have unlocked the key to a dedicated observer, though in those days – with the considerable expense of appropriate literature and the absence of any 'loco cognoscenti' from my circle of acquaintances – knowledge which today would be widely dispersed was in that day much more esoteric. For me, that document was a revelation and might be marked as the starting point in the evolution of my authentic locomotive and railway knowledge.

To my astonishment, there in black type stood all the Scotts, Glens and Directors with names and numbers which I had but partially collected over what to me seemed a lengthy period of observation. Valuable information it was; but lists of numbers were to me merely the index to a whole series of pleasurable episodes wherein I had been in the proximity of these enchanting machines, whose fascination I could not explain to certain bemused relatives or rationalise for my own understanding. The ultimate desire and objective (though imperfectly formulated) was to be in close proximity to or – in the ultimate bliss – travel on one of these machines. The achievement of any such desire was to involve 'tholing' many a year of waiting, before the ultimate achievement.

My first series of systematic railway journeys was made in 1942 whilst working in the British Aluminium Company's works at Burntisland. These were made each morning and evening using a most flexible system of workman's tickets which one bought in weekly sets and thereafter used for either direction of travel, thus avoiding morning and evening queuing at booking office windows.

The morning train was joined at Sinclairtown station at around 7.15 a.m. Both trains used were, essentially, workmen's trains, though not exclusively so. The morning motive power would almost inevitably be a Scott or a Glen and we would watch its familiar profile emerge through the blackened stone arch at the up platform's eastern extremity. Oh! the luxurious comfort of the compartment's steam-heated interior after the morning winds that so often accompanied the short tramp to the station. Within, inevitably, sat the same old faces, and one would listen expectantly to their 'grown-up' gossip.

Being summer, the blackout would have ended and I can recall the rosy glow of the eastern sunrise silhouetting the overbridge and the curious and now vanished, squat, pagoda-like spire of the church which sat atop the station embankment. At Burntisland came the walk to the works gate whilst the multitude of shipyard workers followed their low-level path to the yard. With my associates, bound for our common destination, we first climbed then descended and climbed again. Inside the premises I would watch the following Edinburgh train steam round the curve towards Newbiggin signal box. In the evening the process would be reversed.

Then, at Sinclairtown, the engine would draw right up to the home and distant signals which had a white-painted quadrant board secured to the dark bridge stone-work (to give better definition). I would make my way along the train to gain the exit at the opposite platform-end and so be denied the chance of a last-minute engine scrutiny.

24. British Aluminium Co.'s Peckett saddle tank, in their works. (Photo: Author, c.1948)

Frustratingly, our house lay (in effect) parallel to the railway but separated from it by our road and a large church with tall spire, as well as by the church, glebe and hall between the road and the cutting in which it lay. We were, therefore, aware of all arrivals and departures without ever seeing a train. We would hear expresses whistle from points down the line and, in due course, thunder through the station cutting. Trains for the north we would hear draw into the hidden station and – depending on the time and weather – if listening intently, we might, on occasion hear the slamming of the doors of individual compartments. On many stopping trains, the fireman would operate the blower as soon as the engine stopped, no doubt to maintain a good fire for the subsequent climb beyond Dysart to the summit before Thornton Junction.

Now, we had tall windows in our ground-floor front room (or parlour as it continued to be called long after such rooms had been converted to more modern forms and given more modern appellations). The natural frequency of these deep panes must have coincided with the frequency of note produced by the blower on these engines and a strong sympathetic vibration was induced. Many a time, I feared that a life-time of such vibration would result in a spectacular disintegration, but fortunately such never came and the Intermediates, Scotts and Glens have long since had their blowers silenced for ever. Most possibly, the threatened panes are also consigned to the scrap heap.

On occasion, I would be roused by this alarming signal and would speed down Church Street and along a small cul de sac, where one could view, though in limited fashion, the offending locomotive as it set off for the north, often after the driver had 'wound her back' and set his crank for the maximum starting-torque.

As I sped back to base and more rewarding activities, I would think: 'So near and yet so far.'

Chapter 23

Rail travel in wartime; its impingement on a 'special mission'; morning scurries through Steven Law's Close to the Cowgate and a mathematical objective

September 1943 till December 1945 was my second period of intensive travelling, during which I travelled to and from Edinburgh every weekday with occasional weekends. Once again, my starting point was Sinclairtown station, but the return journeys were mostly made to Kirkcaldy station.

I would generally leave with a train around 7.30 a.m. and return with trains leaving Edinburgh Waverley at 4.20 p.m., 5.10 p.m. or occasionally later. Travel at these times gave much opportunity to observe a wide swathe of railway activity, predominantly of passenger operations but indirectly of freight activity also.

During the latter part of this period, the railway system was under severe pressure, and on occasion timings could be erratic. Frequently the morning train would be late and it was a not infrequent occurrence to leap off the train as soon as it was at a stand, possibly in platform 14 or thereabouts, dash through the barrier as best one could and make for the approach stairs to the overbridge; rush up these stairs, dash along the access gangway (passing the suburban platform exits in the process); rush up the steps to the Market Street station exit; project oneself across the Market Street traffic and, if unscathed, run up the steps by the *Scotsman* premises to emerge into Cockburn Street just below the Tron. Opposite this point of emergence was a short close on a slight incline which gave on to the High Street.

If timing was extremely tight, instead of rushing across the High Street, across the top of Blair Street and thence up the Bridges to enter Chambers Street, we would shoot across the High Street and enter Steven Law's Close, an unsavoury close which passed through the lofty and as yet unrenovated tenement blocks of the Royal Mile. This close ran between high walls to emerge into the Cowgate behind the factory of MacNiven and Cameron (makers of the pens, which were – as many a station hoarding proclaimed – 'A boon and a blessing to men – the Pickwick, the Owl and the Waverley Pen').

Turning sharply through a right angle – if any breath was left in our sorely taxed lungs – we would hurtle right along the Cowgate and infiltrate ourselves into the rear college buildings which faced on to that thoroughfare. We would then face the need to elevate ourselves up a succession of stairs and long corridors to reach the first floor of the Chambers Street Building.

There, we would enter the lecture room, panting and foaming: a sorry spectacle and certainly not one to inspire confidence from the current lecturer. At one stage mathematics was the opening lecture and Mr Read, the lecturer, was not in the slightest impressed by the heroes of the preceding marathon. At one point he even suggested that any repeat performances would result in exclusion from his class, a situation which would have been tantamount to a termination of the course. Somehow or other, we managed to avoid this sudden end of our hopes.

For some reason, he, being from the south, could not conceive of the problems and hazards of arrival in his lecture hall from Fife at 8.55 a.m. prompt, demands on an embattled railway system remaining as they were.

Only two years ago, I attempted the intermediate lap of the 'course' comprising the steps alongside the *Scotsman* premises, and decided – in panting mode – that my fitness must have suffered a dramatic deterioration across the years. In late afternoons (especially after laboratory sessions when the experiment had not gone according to plan) the 'short cut' was not without its problems, but penalties for lateness in that direction might only amount to a very late evening meal.

The occupants of the dwellings above Steven Law's Close seemed, on occasion, to be impelled by deviant tendencies. One colleague just evaded impact from a loaf with which the baker had parted several months before, if hardness and colour were reliable indicators of age. Less savoury materials of an unmentionable liquid form were resorted to; but perhaps specific details are not required in a report that has now deviated far from its intended subject.

Reverting to train timing: one incident stands out clearly in memory. My travelling companions had joined the train well north of Thornton and, from their experience prior to Sinclairtown, predicted a late arrival. The compartment, on reaching Kirkcaldy, was very full and included one passenger who was very agitated by this lateness and became more agitated as the journey proceeded.

The engine was a Scott, as I recall events, and it was obvious that all was not quite well. Quite apart from the condition of the smokebox door, which had been drawing air on some earlier journey, and a minor steam-leak at the dome-joint, the fireman was obviously having steaming problems.

From Kirkcaldy time continued to be lost. After Burntisland, the anxiety of the agitated traveller became quite intense. He had to join a special (military) flight at Turnhouse, he confided in hushed tones, and was well behind his time.

At Aberdour, he could no longer contain himself. As soon as the train stopped he alighted and sought out the stationmaster. There was some delay while they conversed but, together, they eventually made their way to the trim, stone-built signalbox which stood at the east end of the platform. There they entered; and there was obviously a long discussion or phonecall up the line. Eventually he returned and we restarted.

However, the stiff climb to Dalgety Summit was yet another hazard for the poor old Scott, and speed slipped back drastically until we were merely crawling. The rattling of a dart or other irons could be clearly heard and I feared the worst. The poor man was in a dire state of agitation.

There was no happy ending (or dramatic assistance, as my colleagues and I had hoped for at Inverkeithing) though we received normal banking assistance. We arrived very late and the 'anxious one' alighted at Haymarket and sped on foot to the exit – who can guess whither?

Our trials were then still to come.

Chapter 24

Carriage observations of footplatemen; the dire effects of over study

Occasionally on my routine journeys I would find myself in a compartment where footplatemen were already present or had entered to travel 'on the cushions' as they had it. This I always found fascinating and I must admit that I eavesdropped to the maximum extent, to learn as much as I could about their calling.

I recall a group who were reminiscing about some venerable 'old-timer', one of whose habits had been to purchase an evening paper in Edinburgh. He would get set in his corner and devour the contents. When he got the 'right away' he still had much to read and this he appeared to do between signals. These he seemed to locate by sheer experience and the characteristic sounds of the track. He would peruse his paper and – lo and behold! – immediately before the signal, up would come the head, the signal would be observed and action taken. If the board was 'off', down would go the head until just before the next signal and so on until he was well on his way. And he never missed a board. Authentic? Or told to shock an eavesdropper? I know not, but knowing the capabilities of some of these old worthies, I am inclined to treat the tale as authentic.

The tables could be turned, of course. I recall one occasion when I was studying or at least attempting to study (as I most frequently did, of necessity). Simultaneously, I was listening, as hard as I could, to their anecdotes and, obviously, well they knew it.

They started to spin a yarn about some legendary character

who studied so intently that his brain gave up the impossible task, and he became eccentric.

'Ye must have seen him,' says the narrator to his mate, 'Aye hinging aboot the No. 9 platform gate.'

'Aye waitin for somebody that's long died or disappeared.'

'A hopeless case, puir soul.'

'Aye, that's what happens if they dinna watch their step.'

Big winks and grins all round, and a really big wink in my direction which I intercept and all round hilarity follows.

There are some who scorn as hopelessly impractical romantics those who demonstrate an interest in the railways of yesterday.

Such there may be, but, when I look back, it is to a whole way of life and to a body of men who served their generation and their Scottish nation well. A sterling job was done by those men, who knew their calling in every detail and who contributed to the community by their dedication to their task, in some cases not only in their daily task, but in many spheres of valuable activity. For some this involved the advancement of trade-knowledge of their fellows. For others it involved achievement of justice and the sustenance of working conditions for their colleagues.

The sum of such endeavours may not be romantic but it is part of our national railway heritage, which the present should not forget. An analysis of history can so often provide a key to the future. One is tempted to a suspicion that a greater understanding of times past and yesterday's hard-won achievements and difficulties overcome would temper certain of today's instantaneous solutions and lightning theories. Such is not a call to glorify the past for its antiquity alone: rather the antithesis in many instances.

Likewise, in regard to the machines which they used, we should remember the achievements of their designers in the light of the limited knowledge and technology of their time – achievements in most instances of the highest order. Yes, there was a romance in 'steam' but it was a romance encapsulating sterling endeavour in a multiplicity of fields where demands were at maximum with seldom an easy option available.

Chapter 25

Footplate cravings; condign and 'sliding' punishment; risqué juveniles; a Newcastle threat and an alarming leak

As years advanced, my consuming desire was to travel on the footplate. Official means of achieving this proved impossible. Motive power officers seemed to have surrounded themselves with impenetrable fortifications – if indeed their presence and identification could be established in the first place. By the time attempts to seek formal permission had been articulated, it was wartime and this further intensified the difficulties. Several abject missives were eventually despatched; they produced rebuffs that were concise in the extreme but conveyed a clear and absolute negative and a masterly impression that any other attempts at re-application would be foredoomed to final, irrevocable rejection.

To attempt the unauthorised approach seemed equally undesirable and fraught with hazard, especially having been reared in an atmosphere sufficiently Calvanistic as to associate all forms of transgression with dire and condign retribution descending on perpetrators and connivers alike. The major reason for rejecting such attempts was the possibility of reprisal against any compliant or accommodating engine man, as these could imply loss of job and possibly other earnings-related sanctions. It was inbred that to threaten a man's livelihood was a crime of the direst hue. Nonetheless, there was always the vague and irrational hope that somewhere, sometime, a driver would make an offer of access to the footplate.

Access without travel did not seem a crime especially if one was prepared for instant evacuation. Accordingly, I was prone to haunt platforms where there was any likelihood of acquiescence and in any case, how else, I mused in justification, could one acquire any knowledge of locomotive essentials? During student days in Edinburgh, the Waverley station was Mecca and many a precious moment was spent there though few were available and, when snatched, were bought at the price of much running and climbing in lanes and on stairways, much loss of breath and a reduction of already scant mealtime-minutes. For me no hectic common-room minutes at the pontoon school. The headlong rushes were not to that glue-pot but to platform 19 or other such location. My inability at pontoon or last minute acquiral of minimal card-skills were less due to Calvin than to the locomotive. Lack of suitably developed social graces could be jointly attributed to that cause conjointly with study and the crass fear of the dire results of non-application to the perpetual grindstone and daily treadmill.

As a passenger, one acquired a derived but quasi-legitimate access to the presence of the train engine or any other engine sharing a mutual facility. There, I would study and re-study the elegant rocking-shaft/piston-valve-spindle layout of the superheated Scott class engines or ponder on the possible internal arrangement of their snifter valves. There, too, I would trace out and identify the Walschaert Motion elements on the valve gear of a V1 Suburban Tank, a mixed-traffic V2 class or a Gresley Pacific.

Access as an intending passenger in those days had its limitations as passenger accommodation was severely limited and the prime objective of other intending passengers was to secure, and defend to the last, the strategically best seat available. Dalliance in the hallowed presence of the locomotive could imply jammed quarters in the corridor (or engaging in the Philistine practice of leaping out at Haymarket – with like-minded, anti-social travellers – to battle, there, for access to the coaches reserved for passengers forced to travel from that next station, down the line).

I still vividly recall the wintry incident when a student law-breaker, so intentioned, leapt off the decelerating train at Haymarket in his much-practised way but landed on a strategically placed parallel 'slide' made on the platform's ice by some of the unruly, patrician children from one of the Capital's prestigious schools, who commuted from south Fife. That unfortunate, commencing motion at a velocity equal to that of the train at the point of exit, seemed to accelerate so that his final velocity exceeded that of the braking train (as he shot past the engine and down the terminal ramp onto the ballast beyond, amidst a cacophony of asinine catcalls.

A penalty of corridor-travelling might be the presence of some of the said exuberant schoolchildren (of both sexes) who, amongst other high-spirited ploys, demonstrated their advance to adulthood by relating to one another risqué tales – possibly designed to shock fellow travellers of a less-spirited age-group. Truly, one could acquire knowledge even in the corridor of the 4.19 p.m., even though one had to stand for it!

Alas, it is not to be implied that the writer was a paragon of impeccable behaviour on all railway occasions. Determined to find accommodation at all costs, he and a colleague climbed into an apparently empty but engine-less train and awaited action in the corridor, only to be told by the irascible guard that 'he had a good mind to leave us there till the next station – Newcastle'. After all, No. 19 platform (with its through layout) could despatch trains in either direction. Some locomotive-study would have been beneficial in that case; but the guard was not a vengeful man!

A more 'mechanical' recollection of platform 19 relates to a visit to the footplate of a V2 engine at one lunch time. This loco was just about to draw a heavy train south, over the border. This visit illustrated the pressure of war-time conditions. Between the outer and inner backplates, at the outward-facing flanged joint of the firehole-door, a leak had developed and a high-pressure jet of water was shooting across the footplate to strike the tender fall-plate (though the offending orifice was, obviously, of small cross-sectional area). It would be a few years till I stood near a similar jet (from a less crucial source) and that would be on a boiler test-stand.

Chapter 26

Multitudinous journeys from west to east and life in a time of transition

From early 1946 till September 1949, I travelled from and to Glasgow each weekend. Initially, the outward journey commenced on Saturday around 1.06 p.m. and took the direct route to Fife via Winchburgh and Dalmeny; the Sunday evening return involved a change at Edinburgh (Waverley). Eventually, with the introduction of the forty-hour week and an additional Sunday direct-service, both journeys were made by the direct route and the outward journey was made on a Friday evening. This regular pattern of travel was thus maintained over a lengthy period and it will be obvious that the opportunities for the observation of locomotive practice were extensive. Indeed, so many journeys were completed along that route that every feature became engraved on the memory.

As well as the train engines, locomotives could be observed at the termini and – if travelling by Edinburgh – additional opportunity for observation was gratuitously introduced by the line-side parades at both Haymarket and Eastfield engine sheds. Inevitably the train engine was noted and a nostalgic review of the resultant notes makes evocative reading in these non-steam days of Sprinters and 125 traction.

Night-shift working produced further variation in times of travel as did the occasional holiday Monday journeys which were introduced, on occasion, and recourse made to the longer, broken journey via Edinburgh, as the timetable demanded. At one point, also, I took to accompanying a colleague who occasionally returned to his Edinburgh roots, and on such occasions the journey was made via that city. This was made even more deviant by a whim for travel via Bathgate which in those fortunate days implied no additional cost. All of this optional exploration extended the potential for locomotive observation.

In the Bathgate ventures, the locomotive sheds of Parkhead, Kipps and Bathgate were surveyed in passing, and a window opened on the coal and iron heartlands of Lanarkshire in addition to the coal and shale-fields of West Lothian. I was thereby having a long-deferred 'practical' or tutorial on the geography lessons of primary-school days, and half-forgotten names became endowed with the reality of direct scrutiny, however grim such might be. Mineral traffic was axiomatic in these parts and, consequentially, freight engines were in some profusion. As enthusiasts, if not students, of these machines, these were exciting byways.

Not being driven by the dedication of the train spotter, no intensive note taking was applied; nor were many of our journeys of the calibre and timing which would give reign to the complex, systematic analysis of the dedicated student of locomotive practice and performance, even had we been provided with the prerequisite equipment and endowed with the analytical techniques demanded by such detailed scrutiny. Journeys for me were embarked on to reach a destination with minimum practical delay, and work demands at all times called the tune. In that period, Work was god and all else had to be subservient. Priorities were well-established and if locomotives had to be observed, then that observation had to be fitted into a rigidly fixed scale of priorities.

In later days, when 'work' would, tantalisingly, thrust the by-product of 'business-journeys' into the pattern of life and there would be rail travel to the industrial activities of the Tyne, the Midlands, London and the south, not to mention brief spells abroad, the self-imposed work-schedule would dominate, and time for scrutiny of the travel-scene would be fragmentary and residual in nature. Such ventures were far down the road of life and meantime Monklands or Bathgate would be the only 'exotic' realms traversed.

At the late stage of penning this, however, it is tantalising in the extreme to observe the sheer paucity of the notes and contemplate the exotica – by today's scale of observation – which might have graced these pages. How marvellous it was, nonetheless, to have been alive at that time, to witness that last age of the active steam locomotive (and no less the first tentative, partially-blundering steps into the subsequent traction era). The railway was still a fundamental element in the nation's life and still held promise of a future, however different from the contemporaneous regime its form might take. The dire hand of conviction-politics had not yet been laid upon it and many railway men, indeed, were to look to the coming nationalisation as a great time of vindication and expansion for the system, based on impartial analysis of needs and means.

None could visualise at that period the dire forces of naked greed and prejudice that would utilise the might of politics, to shake the foundations of the industry some thirty years thereafter.

No such dire thoughts clouded the dream then, however, and, like Wordsworth of old: 'Great was it in that dawn to be alive; but to be young was very heaven.'

If I am adjudged (by myself – certainly and by the world most probably) to have at the end of the day achieved nothing, then such an assessment ignores the sheer joy and enthusiasm of those days and the opportunity to work and yarn with the men who designed, made and ran engines, whose daily tasks kept the railways moving, and amongst whom were some visionaries who looked beyond the current idiom to new ways both technical and sociological.

This is no glorification of the past merely for the past, which was sorely imperfect, as even the most imperceptive would concede; but it was, at least for some, a time of vision, for what might yet be. It certainly was a time when it was not thought insane to have an enthusiasm for work, especially if it was work on locomotives (which must rank amongst the most fascinating of man's creations).

Chapter 27

Sixteen years of railway observations in retrospect: 'Glen Loy' in tunnel difficulties; 'Meg Dodds' in need of assistance; 'Dandie Dinmont' as a Castlecary casualty

It is of some retrospective interest to view the gradual changes in motive power over the years 1946 till 1962, as indicated by the limited information jotted down as peripheral or incidental notes to my daily diary entry which was of a severely truncated form and basically a journal of work and study, with an appended, rudimentary and highly-compressed record of certain non-work activities (few of which today would be defined as recreational).

A survey of 1946 shows a remarkably traditional provision of engines in what is, in essence, a record of Kirkcaldy to Glasgow travel and the associated return-journeys (with a few Kirkcaldy/Waverley and Waverley/Queen Street journeys when shift-working changed the weekend programme).

The main traction burden of that portion of the Fife/Glasgow/Fife service seemed to have been borne by a combination of Scotts, Glens and Directors. Only one B1 was recorded – an early member of the Antelope family (Roedeer No. 1040, in pristine condition, ex Queens Park Works, for public preview, to which I had made an evening visit to Queen Street Station on Monday evening of 29th April 1946).

One Intermediate was noted – No. 9886 – whilst among the Scotts and Glens were some of the old familiar names from the halcyon days of boyhood observation on Tayside and in South Fife, including 'Glen Nevis', 'Glen Ogle' and 'Glen Gloy', not to mention 'Glen Loy' who had produced for me and my fellow passengers a few alarmingly dubious moments several years before, in Ferryhills tunnel when she 'lost her feet' near 'the top end' and seemed to be more prone to go backwards than forward, and out of the enshrouding total darkness rearwards. It was even more alarming for those who in that day – before the sand-drag later provided – were aware of the catch-points at the tunnel-mouth.

25. Glen Gloy' at Thornton. Built June 1920; withdrawn 1960. Tractive effort 22,100 lb. (Photo given to author by the late Mr James Brown)

'Simon Glover' was amongst the group, and of it I have the most lucid initial recollection, as it steamed atop the embankment *c.*1934 at Leuchars Lodge *en route* for the Tay Bridge and Dundee. Also included was 'Dirk Hatteraick', which was the second engine I photographed with my aunt's Kodak Brownie camera, when it was on a 'trip-working' turn at Tayport Harbour, possibly in the summer of 1939.

'Meg Dodds' was another old familiar name but on the Saturday recorded she had been in trouble, as a pilot, in the form of J35 (No. 9366), had been called upon to bank her from Inverkeithing all the way to Kirkcaldy).

Also recorded was 'Dandie Dinmont' (9896), the rear of whose train was run into by 'Grand Parade' on a snowy day near Castlecary in 1937.

Chapter 28

Weekly locomotive observations in 1948–9; less regular sightings in 1951–2 on the Sunday evening train from Fife to Glasgow; Random observations in 1952–3; A memory of 'Glen Beasdale'

Although there were no dramatic changes in the observations of 1948-9 the signs of minor changes could be discerned. One such was the growth period for 'B1' usage and in this highly limited observation, nine instances of B1 haulage were recorded, including one with Strang Steel.

Shires were becoming decidedly noticeable with appearances by 'Aberdeenshire', Banffshire', 'Berwickshire', 'Cheshire', 'Dunbartonshire', 'Stirlingshire' and 'Northumberland'.

As in the previous period, Directors were well represented with long-remembered names such as 'The Lady of the Lake', 'Ellen Douglas', 'Lord Glenallan', and 'Allan Bane', all bringing with them visions of summer Tayside days with their bearers, perhaps nosing through the Shanwell overbridge, emerging from the Commonty Cutting with mighty reverberations, or heading for the West Light of a twilight evening with the rods ringing as only those of Gresley's creations could.

But the ranks of the Scotts and Glens were still impressive, even though presenting a diminishing presence. Scotts 'Simon Glover' and 'Dirk Hatteraick' as well as 'Glen Murran' were still steaming on and all redolent of the happy scenes of yesterday. In 1949 the B1 presence consolidated further with thirteen appearances including 'Alexander Reith Gray'. 'Perthshire' also appeared as a representative of her class. Amazingly, two Intermediates were recorded (62451 and 62460). And certain

26. NBR Scott class of W.P. Reid design in LNER days. 'Dirk Hatteraick', built at Cowlairs, December 1911. Shunting at Tayport harbour after evening trip working from Leuchars. Withdrawn September 1950. Tractive effort 19,434 lb. (Photo: Author, c.1938)

further Scotts and Glens held their place: 'Kettledrummle' and 'Guy Mannering' amongst them, as was 'Glen Orchy'.

As always, the Directors were well represented with warriors 'Colonel Gardiner' and 'Captain Craigengelt' as well as 'Baron Bradwardine' amongst their ranks.

1950 saw the B1s hold their own, in my very journey-specific and unscientific survey. But 'Impala' was there with impeccable credentials. 'Cheshire' appeared twice, together with 'Roxburgh', 'Rutland' and 'Northumberland' to demonstrate persistent Shire Class presence. Yet again, the Directors were steady visitors with 'Maid of Lorn', 'Flora MacIvor', 'Jonathan Oldbuck' and 'Roderick Dhu', which were but some of that long-remembered breed performing. Likewise still steaming were a number of Scotts, 'Meg Dodds', 'The Pirate' and 'The Abbot' amongst them, as well as the indefatigable Glens: 'Quoich', 'Finnan' and 'Gloy' to name a few. But there was one 'new' performer in the shape of 'Stanier' (45697) from Waverley to Queen Street on 1 March 1950. One journey from Sinclairtown to Waverley was made behind a J39.

A very unprofessional analysis of a very limited 'sample' in 1951 showed 19.6 per cent observed journeys dealt with by B1s; 41.2 per cent Director-hauled; 11.2 per cent behind Shires. Glens made a showing on 9.8 per cent of journeys and Scotts on 8.4 per cent with one solitary Intermediate appearance (62475).

One interesting appearance was that of V4 class 'Bantam Cock's' sister engine, known in our neck of the woods – inevitably – as 'Bantam Hen'. Sad it was that fate did not allow the master to develop this new class and that only two should be built. Amongst the steady Director appearances was that of 'Haystoun of Bucklaw' (62682); whose proportions from a line-side proximity in Thornton Shed had so impressed me back in 1945.

In the year of 1952 there came a decided change, not only in my viewing opportunities. At the beginning of June I got married and took up house in Glasgow. Any continuity in the locomotive record is thus diminished (if not negated for statistical purposes, supposing that so far any acceptable base did exist for any mathematical or statistically purist reader).

For the latter part of the year, the 7.37 p.m. (Sunday evening) from Kirkcaldy knew me not again as a regular supporter. For sporadic further journeys, however, the Directors, as ever, hogged much of the limelight, with the Shires putting in frequent appearances.

New blood was injected at this point with the coming of Standard Class 4s which made their debut (43135 and 43137 in particular). There was a small B1 appearance. This is possibly a distortion of actuality, as I must reiterate that locomotive data was not recorded on all journeys otherwise the authenticity and volume of the data would have been much more profound. Friday evening journeys were not recorded, possibly owing to an extreme urgency to meet my 'beloved', who normally came to meet that train. B1s were very consistent performers on the Friday evening train as it so happened.

A Class 5 put in an appearance on Sunday evening of 23 March which may have presaged things yet to come. But 'Glen Beasdale' appeared on Sunday evening 24 February, as an old faithful friend. She evinces a vignette of a very sunny summer afternoon at Tayport station with the 2.41 p.m. train awaiting departure with 'Glen Beasdale' at its head and simmering in the heat. The 2.35 p.m. for St Andrews is crossing the above down train, after passage of the tablet to the signal man on his wooden staging. The driver has left his engine and is resting his legs, just to the left of the tunnel-like station entrance. How that sun shone; and how intensely happy was I, a youthful and enthusiastic observer of that long-forgotten ritual.

On 21 June, I happened to be travelling from Waverley, and at the head of the train was A4 – 'Empire of India'. Later, Tayport was visited in late September, and on our way home from Dundee (West) we had no less an engine than the short-lived BR standard locomotive 'Clan Campbell' drawing our train. Things were changing all round.

Travelling did not cease (merely diminished) in 1952, whilst the year 1953 saw regular visits to relatives and friends in the Kingdom of Fife. That year saw our summer holiday spent there, and July saw us heading back from Newburgh to Ladybank behind a Pickersgill 4-4-0 (on a branch whose last days saw not a few ex-Caley locomotives including the odd Caley Jumbo, such as we noted while exploring at Abernethy one afternoon. We were alerted by smoke and steam afar off, beyond Aberargie; and thereafter we traced its passage across the plain from the Bridge of Earn region to the elevated, timber platform of the erstwhile Pictish capital.

Chapter 29

To view Old Sarum and Stonehenge and discuss locos with an SR driver; to ponder over the nature of the Strong Country

In a survey of locomotive experiences, perhaps that engendering the maximum frustration relates to an experience at Paddington Station in the early autumn of 1950. At that time, I had been sent on a course, of several weeks' duration, to the School of Gas Turbine Technology located at Farnborough. Because of some administrative hitch, I was given no prior notice of this arrangement and had to depart from Glasgow with literally only a few hours warning: just sufficient to enable a panic call to home for some additional clothing as I had planned to return thither at the coming weekend.

The course (which proved to be extremely interesting and useful) was naturally an intense one, but there was no weekend instruction. Those with homes or friends in London or the Home Counties betook themselves to these locations. Midland venues would no doubt have also been practicable but to return to Scotland was not a sustainable proposition. I was thus able to carry out some exploration of destinations readily accessible by rail.

On one of the Saturdays, I travelled to Salisbury, whose Cathedral, not to mention spire and close, as well as town and environs, made a profound and lasting impression. I also walked out to Stonehenge from Amesbury, which produced no less a fascinating recollection. This journey was, of course, made by the Southern Railway main line to the south-west. Many a time, I had read descriptions of its operation and had scrutinised

27. Wareham, west of Bournemouth in June 1952. A. Mansell's Lord Nelson Class locomotive, built 1926–9. Tractive effort 33,510 lb.

pictures in such publications as the *Railway Magazine* and *Meccano Magazine* of its salient locations and the locomotives which performed sterling service there, against these backgrounds. How often had I seen such in the columns of the latter in early days, or in the pages of the former of later times.

It was with a real feeling of achievement that I sped from Farnborough to Salisbury on one of these track stretches, which had been subconsciously marked down as future beckoning challenges (as the mountain climber of today, no doubt, casts an eye on some remote Munro).

With intense expectation, I scanned that railway scene for some vision of a 'Merchant Navy', some Lord Nelson or even – though much less likely, I reasoned – some Drummond creation or loco of comparable vintage.

The whole countryside was simultaneously scrutinised and the impressions derived continuously weighed against a composite standard of early images from a host of sources which constituted my preconception of southern rural England. This unlikely compound was synthesised from such incompatibles as

Thomas Hardy, Charles Dickens, encyclopaedic children's works by Arthur Mee, railway literature – both commercial and amateur – and a bountiful swatch of 'school' and other tales avidly selected in formative years from the shelves of my local children's library. Distance had given imagination fancy free range and the concept of that southern countryside was possibly widely deviant from reality.

Nonetheless, I found the land of green fields and spreading woods not too much at variance with my romanticised notions, especially in that now distant era, which had not been disrupted by the vast and in some cases cataclysmic changes which were yet to break upon it. These were, no doubt, the last days of the rural railway, with motor-ways and the by-passes which they spawn still to tear, rend and scarify the countryside. Possibly, too, these were the twilight times of the local breweries. So, bemused, I awaited the 'Strong Country' and on arrival speculated on those aspects of this promised land which might be stronger than that just left.

I had left my starting point with the 8.45 a.m. from Farnborough and had changed at Basingstoke to catch the Salisbury and south-west train. At my destination, I had a long discussion with the driver of the local train on locomotive matters and more specifically on local practice and performance. It seemed that no matter where one found oneself, the railway and all its attributes, especially the locomotives and their acolytes, made a common bond with one's own locality, which eliminated any sense of isolation and provided a common language and a universal enthusiasm, of amateurs and professionals alike. This, for me, was demonstrated to an extreme extent some years later, when the crew of a Deutsche Bundesbahn Tank at Friedrichshafen invited me on to their footplate and in a mixture of tongues sought with great enthusiasm to indicate the mysteries of their Bremse Zettel!

A rejected opportunity; magnificent, resplendent and discarded London termini; a remembrance of Flanders and the rivers; the Victorian way of death buried by arboreal explosion

On the following day, Sunday, I stepped aboard the 10.29 morning train to Waterloo, and at that terminus took a tube to Paddington. After appraising the magnificent conception of the founding fathers embodied in that vast structure, I made my way to the extremity of a platform, where my eye had lighted upon a Castle class locomotive.

To my delight I was invited on to the footplate, where a long discussion ensued with the driver on a wide-ranging spread of locomotive topics, but with pertinent reference to Great Western practice and more specifically to these fine machines, which had set a marker in the unfolding history of locomotive development. Who knows how long this discussion might

28. 'Drysllwyn Castle'. Originally it was numbered 5076; that photographed may originally have been 5051 'Earl Bathurst' for period 1936-63. No. 7081 was named 'Drysllwyn Castle' 1949–63. Class introduced 1923. Tractive effort 31,625 lb. (Photo: J.A. Macleod at Didcot Great Western Society premises on 26 September 1982)

have lasted if untrammelled, but departure time was fast approaching.

With total incredulity, I heard the driver ask if I would care to travel with him to Oxford. With something akin to unbelief I heard myself mumble in the negative. With my restricted wardrobe, I feared that I would not be able to withstand the consequences of any grime and dishevelment that might befall me on that coveted journey. Proffering a heartfelt acknowledgement of this incredible offer, I stepped down on to that platform with a gloom born of frustration and the awareness of the total unlikelihood of such incredible fortune being repeated. No doubt I sought to rationalise my response in moral terms but that missed opportunity is mourned as deeply now as it was then – more especially as the equivalent circumstances can never now return.

With thoughts on the legendary greatness of the Great Western and the great names of Gooch, Brunel, Churchward and Hawksworth dominating my thoughts, I felt impelled to linger and spent not a little time viewing some modern GWR engines from the vantage point of the platform. The other railway empire, with which till then I had had no contact, was the Great Eastern, whose posters I recalled from early childhood, in vintage LNER coaching stock. The Great Eastern Hotel at Liverpool Street had been publicised as a Mecca for discriminating travellers and had possibly induced some latent objective to view this centre of reputed luxury and elegance. My desire, now, was not to view the hotel but, rather, the station, the operation of whose commuter traffic in the days of small steam locomotives and manual signalling had been a token to the powers of human organisation and resource. These facilities, no doubt adjudged crude and primitive by today's standards, had effectively handled massive movements of people between suburbs and city with incredible efficiency.

The site of such herculean endeavours, had to be seen! There, too, 'Sandringhams' might be espied and these were for me living legends, being machines which had graced the pages of my childhood's railway books; they had been constructed in Hyde Park and had been accepted for the LNER, on that site, by Bob Fairgrieve himself (the tales of which operation I had heard so often).

Paddington was not left, however, before first having a lengthy yarn with the fireman of another Castle class locomotive. A further tube-journey was then made to Piccadilly, as my only eating-house recollections had been of that spot on my very first visit to London. A speedy turn-round had then been provided at that establishment and speed was of the essence. After all, eating was but a necessary evil in the immediate scale of priorities on that safari! Added to which, I knew of no other obvious facilities.

After a satisfactory meal, a tube was taken to Blackfriars and from there on foot the route was along the Embankment and across Hungerford Bridge at the southern extremity of which the site of the Festival of Britain was viewed. The ultimate destination was, of course, Waterloo Station. On arrival the opportunity was taken to examine in some detail engines which till then had, of necessity, merely been shot a hurried glance in passing. Several tank engines were thus studied, certain of which had presented a somewhat archaic impression, due in no small measure to the presence of their dome-mounted safety valves. Paradoxically, these features seemed somehow out of context on a system which was characterised by its wide and spreading electrification, its current active speculation on dieselisation and such impressive milestones in its locomotive progression as the Lord Nelson Class, the King Arthurs and the Schools Class, not to mention the stimulating design approach of Bulleid's Merchant Navy Class and, now, his West Country Class.

The dome-mounted safety valves were redolent of 'Dugald Drummond' and thus of home.

Such out-of-context presences seemed to negate the awesomeness of the capital city and to disclose some of its more mundane and homely aspects behind the grand façade – foolish illusions, no doubt.

A particularly remembered locomotive was of Drummond's M7 class for the LSWR (0-4-4 Tank engines built between 1896 and 1911) and, there, simmered such a machine, at the platform-end, by the ticket barrier in 1950 and still steaming effectively in the dawning era – as we fervently hoped – of the gas-turbine locomotive concept.

Another particularly remembered engine was a 4-4-0, with whose crew I became involved in a long and fascinating conversation. Stupidly, I mistook the vertically-mounted steam-reverser for the Westinghouse air compressor and was corrected by them. The exact engine-type can no longer be specified, with certainty, as I made no notes of these events and so imposed a burden on memory, which I apparently dismissed as an unrealistic non-problem – as it still indubitably was, then. I strongly believe that the class could have been of SECR origin, of a type originally built by Stirling and designated class symbol B1. Any reader who has progressed this far is left to contemplate the likely authenticity of such a diagnosis.

After maximum absorption of the Waterloo theme, a further tube was taken, this time to Liverpool Street Station, as earlier planned at Paddington. On that particular Sunday, it was a somewhat dingy spot, certainly if it were to be compared with the magnificent re-creation of early glories which have been carried out of late, with impressive and inspiring results. Here, however, lay a virgin seam and a currently little-known territory. The Scandinavian was much in evidence and at its head a Sandringham class locomotive no less! This vision was advanced upon with alacrity and in no time at all I was involved in a prolonged and fascinating discussion with the fireman.

Above Liverpool Street, I was aware, lay Broad Street Station, which in its time had seen and, no doubt, echoed to the locomotives of J.C. Park (he of the hollow-bored firebox-stays and several other worthy locomotive features). A glimpse at the old North London terminus seemed imperative and so in that direction, after a thorough assessment of the Great Eastern scene, I turned my steps, only to find that it was closed (no doubt as it was the Sabbath).

Euston demanded attention, not least because a sleeper booking was desirable for the homeward journey in one week's time; but also for the locomotive delights that might be lurking there. Somehow *en route*, however, Moorgate was encompassed and, there, lo and behold! I saw an old engine of the City and South London Railway, dated 1906.

From Euston (reservations and exploration complete), I made my way back to Waterloo, for the return to Farnborough on the 5.45 p.m. To my great delight, the train engine was no other than 'Remembrance' an evocative picture of which, I recalled as having been scanned in that visual and printed cornucopia of awakening images that had been Sinclairtown children's library of earlier days.

So, with an engine of renown at our head (a 1934 rebuild from the large but ill-fated 4.6.4 River Class 'Tanks', as I recalled), we drew out of Waterloo in the pale light of early evening, with the cityscape spreading to the south-east, on a route that was becoming familiar, though no longer with the element of awe that is engendered when setting out for the unknown, as on that initial Surrey-bound journey in the opening days of 1946.

Certain landmarks were now sought out (gone though they now are; and certainly not to be seen by today's commuter. For gone is the large Doulton factory building with its façade made prominent by those facing ceramics redolent of Victorian Civic Fountains and other such architectural wonders). Such a wonder as in Kelvingrove – stands stranded after the exhibition which espoused it has for ever vanished in the mists of time. Gone, also, is its great ornamental chimney stalk, like that other anachronism no longer seen downstream, the Lead-Shott Tower.

Later came that comparable curiosity in kiln form and bearing the name of Brand of meat extract or essence fame. Irrational as it was, one speculated on some weird Liebig condenser, still winning back the last drop of concentrated vitamin from the boiling of some prime beef concentrate.

Much later came a vast seeds-man firm, after a wide common, and away down the line – in Surrey, no doubt – the unbelievable, sprawling, tree-encircled acres of Brookwood Cemetery and its visions of these agony-filled funeral trains steaming down from Waterloo with all their Victorian symbols of death and the ultimate departure. The cemetery is, possibly, still there; and if similar graveyards elsewhere are typical, possibly raising immense problems of ownership, maintenance and running costs. No doubt, however, the Victorian reliquary is now mostly hid from the hurrying commuters, too obsessed and depressed, if not driven suicidal by the commercial problems of the moment, to be aware of the agony and the tragedies of yesterday, mercifully smothered, perhaps, by rank vegetation and arboreal explosion.

Back to Farnborough by the LSWR Main Line

In due course, we crossed the now-familiar bridge, straddling a north–south line which passed beneath and at a right angle to that main SR artery, *en route* to North Camp and thence Aldershot to the south-west (circumscribing the wood-crowned hill behind the school). Immediately after that sighting, we passed under the arched foot-bridge preceding Farnborough Station, which must have been located above the four parallel tracks (up and down fast and slow lines) by someone who wished to provide the ultimate experience for students of LSWR locomotive practice.

Details may fade; but the inherently stimulating experiences of that weekend will never be completely eradicated.

Gone for ever is the possibility of observing these fine machines in their inimitable and operationally co-eval environs. Silent, now, will have fallen most of the tongues of those with whom were shared those discussions of engines and enginemen, and from whom came these yarns which generated so much mutual pleasure (in pride of craft and calling). Their day was even then closing. New modes of traction were even then being discussed, although with open minds on all sides and great expectancy. Few, however, could conceive the unknown perils which were yet to engulf the industry to which they had given their all.

The tide of new technology was already washing up a diminishing strand: not, we had universally thought, a threatening tide, but one which could even bring better conditions and, through new ways, could provide rebirth and predominance of an old but noble industry which had served its nation well. As the day's discussions had revealed, there was an eager desire to grasp the new whilst revering the old, with all its history of conquest over dire challenges, by preceding generations.

None would have conceived that that indigenous technology and engineering, which held great promise of advance and betterment, would be spurned by the politicians of thirty years later and that strange and confused shibboleths would reduce their industry to a truncated, mutilated, debased and enervated relic shorn of its potential as an energy-conserving, environment-enhancing, vital artery of trade and communication.

CHAPTER 30

Sundry observations in 1953; the prime of the Scots Directors; English travel greatly expands

My recorded rail journeys of 1953 were few in number, certainly in comparison with previous years, as, with my own home, now in Glasgow, the opportunities or necessity for regular travel had much diminished; those journeys recorded reflecting journeys to visit relations in Fife.

A new opportunity for travel was presenting itself in the form of business journeys and these were to expand considerably in the ensuing years and must eventually have represented a considerable rail mileage. Business and recording were not altogether compatible and a most fruitful seam was not exploited especially as there were many journeys across the years: to the south, with the longest possibly that to Swansea via Crewe, Shrewsbury and the Mid Wales route as well as the ensuing homeward-journey via the Severn tunnel to London and thence from Euston to Glasgow Central. In due course points reached included Erith, Ashford and Maidstone in Kent, Colchester, Harwich, Brighton, Eastbourne; Rugby (many times) and Birmingham (likewise); Bedford, Manchester, Farnborough, Bristol, Nuneaton (several times), Coventry; Melton Mowbray via Nottingham; Newcastle (on a very large number of occasions); Preston for Leyland; Harrogate (several times); Winnington; Edinburgh (for Lady Victoria Colliery); Ayr and Aberdeen (several times).

London was visited on a considerable number of occasions, including, very many years later, Dartford and Sommerstown. Many journeys were made by night and thus rendered observation impossible. Certain were made in the company of others and that, naturally, narrowed the scope for observation considerably.

Five recorded journeys were made in 1953 with the 'old' Sunday evening train when returning after visits to the Lang Toun, and it was interesting to note that B1s (including 'Sir Harold Mitchell' on two journeys) accounted for three journeys in total whilst Directors – 'Ellen Douglass' and 'Baron of Bradwardine' – provided the motive power on the remainder. However, it may be observed that Kitson's and Armstrong Whitworth only commenced turning out their orders for the Scots Directors around the autumn of 1924. These engines must have been in their prime (age-wise) when they first drew my attention, and at that age considerably younger than Reid's NBR 4-4-0s. Of these, the Intermediates were introduced in 1907 and the first batch of Scott class engines in 1909 (including 'Dandie Dinmont'.

29. LNER D11/2 modified 'Director' Class locomotive No. 61291: 'Luckie Mucklebackit'. Tractive effort 19,644 lb. (Photo: the late James Beveridge, Guardbridge)

The second batch, of which 'Dirk Hatteraick', 'Ivanhoe', 'Guy Mannering' and 'Lady of Avenel' were part, were built in 1911. The ultimate superheated batch, including 'Meg Dodds', 'Kettledrummle', 'The Pirate', 'The Abbot' and 'Jingling Geordie', came some years later. The first Glen – 'Glen Finnan' – was placed in service in 1913.

Several journeys were made from Glasgow to Tayport and time considerations made it imperative on the outward journey to take the Caley route to Dundee (West), a route with which, at that period, I had only become acquainted in the previous two years, with some two journeys at the New Year Break when my family were wont to forgather there and bring in the New Year in the company of my aunt (and my uncle prior to his death in 1941).

The Buchanan Street to Dundee (West) journey was to become much better known to me in years to come and its engines likewise. In 1953, my three recorded journeys over that route recorded a Black Five as providing the motive power on each occasion (which, indubitably, one would expect).

In that year another familiar journey was made (on 27th July) during our summer break, as a repeat of the old Newburgh to Ladybank routine. A Caley Pickersgill 4-4-0 once again hauled the train, and yet again confirmed my view that these were well-proportioned locomotives. Paradoxically my first introduction to this class had been on a very early exploration of St Enoch's Station, in the innocent belief that GSWR locomotives could still be observed in the cathedral-like vastness of that terminus.

CHAPTER 31

1954 experiences: Preston for Leyland; the delights of Darvel, Kilmarnock and Ayr; re-seeking the joys of Callander; a Ladybank–Newburgh–Inverness safari

Of the 1954 journeys recorded, only the briefest of notes survive and these for a mere twenty-seven trips.

One recording (contrary to earlier comments) refers to a work-orientated journey to Preston on a visit to discuss the adoption of a Leyland industrial diesel engine for the auxiliary generator drive on the Coal-Burning Gas-turbine-Locomotive Project. To achieve this I travelled with the 4.05 p.m. train from Glasgow Central (on 13th September 1954) when we had one of the British Railways standard locomotives 'Clan Macdonald' at our head, a class only introduced in 1952 to a Derby design with 6'2" driving wheels and a boiler pressed to 225 psig. Returning from Preston next day (with the 5.30 p.m.) the motive power was an LMS Jubilee, of Stanier 1934 design, 'Irresistible' (and Glasgow Central was reached at 9.27 p.m.).

Now settled in Glasgow, we were wont to do a fair measure of weekend exploration, the facilities for which were excellent in those days. Most, if not all, of these Saturday afternoon forays to a wide range of destinations, were made by train. Once again a great potential for recording performance details was lost, but domestic contact was already minimised by the increasing demands of work, and to introduce further erosion during leisure moments, in the guise of amateur locomotive studies, was intolerable.

We had little knowledge of Ayrshire and recently had received random reports of sundry visits to that airt from a number of acquaintances. An instantaneous decision was reached one Saturday noon that we should explore Kilmarnock and the Irvine Valley. St Enoch's was thus visited and the 2.00 p.m. train boarded for Kilmarnock on 24th September. After a very brief assessment of the main shopping area (a natural hazard on all such excursions), the 3.54 p.m. train to Darvel was boarded and the adjacent, line-side regions by Hurlford and the lace-manufacturing towns of Galston and Newmilns observed.

On arrival at Darvel, the deserted nature of the town suggested that the whole population had expired or had left for Kilmarnock with the previous train. Assuming the latter explanation, we followed suit (though in fairness to the good people of Darvel it must be said that the weather was poor and the day grey and overcast as well as cold to boot). A curious glance was cast further east along the valley in the direction of the line to Muirkirk but little was to be seen of that route to Lanark and the east.

I recall that the motive power for our trip up and down the branch was a 2-6-4 tank but of precise details, none remain. After further exploration of Kilmarnock and suitable refreshment, the 7.08 p.m. train was taken back to St Enoch's with 'Cameronian' at the head. (Truly a sign of changing times to see a Gresley Pacific on 'Soo West' territory.)

In September a further foray was made into Ayrshire, when friends were visited in Prestwick on Saturday 18th and Ayr was explored in their company. The 13.30 p.m. ex St Enoch was our outward train and return was by 9.39 p.m. from Prestwick. In both directions the locomotive was a BR standard 2-6-4 tank. St Enoch's was reached at 10.56 p.m. on our return.

Earlier, on 20th August, nostalgia ruled and an excursion was taken to Callander with the 10.15 a.m. from Buchanan Street, returning with the 5.25 p.m. from Callander and 6.24 p.m. from Stirling. To my surprise, the unexpected train engine (of NBR design) between Stirling and Callander was no other than 'Glen Lyon'.

Part of our summer holiday of that year, was spent in Newburgh and a journey is recorded (behind another Caley Pickersgill 4-4-0) to that destination – from Ladybank.

While on holiday there, however, we travelled from Perth to Inverness, returning on Saturday (24th July) with the 5.15 p.m. behind two Black Fives, and reaching Perth five minutes early.

Tayport had also received a visit and from thence I made my first journey between St Andrews and Crail, the return portion of which was made on that Saturday evening 31st August behind a B1 Class locomotive). By then the possibilities of a repetition were becoming severely limited.

An earlier journey on 16th May is recorded from Tayport, behind a B1 Class engine (No. 61263) – a well-known performer in those parts.

30. LMS 'Jubilee' Class Mysore, sister engine to Keppell. (Valentine postcard, purchased 1939)

The remainder of the records for 1954 divide between the Glasgow/Dundee and Glasgow/Kirkcaldy routes. An interesting entry relating to the former route is of 'Keppell' (an ex LMS Jubilee class locomotive rostered on 5th January), while the remaining motive power is exclusively of Class 5 provision.

On the old familiar Fife/Glasgow Sunday evening run, the division of motive power provided seemed to indicate a majority of B1 Class locomotives, with familiar numbers: 61263; 61103; 61277 and 61064 included. Two exceptions, however, were Director hauled (old acquaintances both: 'Maid of Lorn' and 'Lord James of Douglas').

On 16th May Shire Class locomotive 'Stirlingshire' provided the traction.

CHAPTER 32

A testing visit to Colchester; routine recordings from 1955; a melancholy Pickersgill farewell

My diary for 1955 gives a listing of only twenty-four rail journeys, but a small number are in the interesting category. One such records a sighting, while passing Sighthill Goods Yard in late February. There, I had espied locomotive No. 1 of Messrs Bairds and Scottish Steel, in transit and no doubt under tow to some maintenance location. This was a most interesting engine, which from time to time could be sighted on the old Monkland and Kirkintilloch line, near Garngaber Junction (to the East of Lenzie), possibly hauling coal or coke for its owners' blast furnaces at Gartsherrie, by Coatbridge. It carried a plate indicating that it was authorised by the Railway Executive to operate over their tracks.

At one point, I can recall it being in Hyde Park erecting shop for overhaul. It had been purchased from an English railway initially but, regrettably, I have forgotten the pertinent details. It had a most impressive dome (or dome cover), which I recall as being of polished brass.

Baird's had many coal pits as well as a coke-oven plant (known locally as 'The Gold Mine') around Kilsyth.

One work-related journey is recorded between Euston and Glasgow Central (on 16th July), when the locomotive (on the 9.10 p.m.) was a Stanier Pacific 'Duchess of Atholl' and Central Station was reached at 6.10 a.m.

I had returned from a week-long assignment, witnessing running tests on a 200 hp Paxman diesel engine from a diesel-shunting locomotive. The journey to Colchester had involved an overnight journey from Perth on the Sunday evening (behind an unrecorded Duchess), having spent a weekend with my wife at Tayport (which I had reached by travelling with the 6.10 p.m. ex Buchanan Street on the Friday evening). Euston had been reached at 7.35 a.m. on Monday morning and a tube taken to Moorgate: to catch the 8.30 a.m. at Liverpool Street.

This must have been one of my most intense travel spasms. The engine-calibration operation had initially been planned for completion on the following Friday, but it was 5.30 on Friday evening when I reached Colchester station, just in time to catch the London train. (Thereby hangs a hectic week-long tale – but that is dealt with elsewhere.)

By that time I was, theoretically, on holiday (as it was, by then Glasgow Fair Friday evening). However, a tube was taken to Euston from Liverpool Street where – as luck had it – I was able to book a sleeper at the last moment and make a phone call to indicate my plans.

Arriving at Glasgow Central Station at 6.10 a.m., I grabbed a taxi and rapidly collected my holiday luggage, my wife having stayed over in Tayport during my absence. In due course a trolley-bus took me to Buchanan Street Station, where I joined a traditionally high-spirited milling mob, all set in going 'aff for the Fair'.

At 9.15 a.m., I was leaving Buchanan Street and at 11.38 a.m. joined the Tayport local. It was not perhaps surprising that I was unable to record detailed travel data in relation to traction encountered. Who said that rapid transit would be impossible without the car and the plane?

While at Tayport a rail journey was made to St Andrews by the 'old' time-honoured 2.35 p.m. train, a B1 at its head. This same motive power brought us back from the Old Grey City, with the 8.34 p.m. (ex Thornton). Whilst at St Andrews Station, Glen Murran was noted on a train. The ultimate return was by the long-remembered route to Kirkcaldy by the direct, original line to Leuchars; and thence south. The motive power, in the form of a K2 locomotive, was a deviation from the inevitable NBR presence, so often noted on that route in days of yore.

In the months thereafter, however, several weekends were spent in Tayport. That summer is recalled for the amazing and possibly unexcelled weather whose arrival was heralded in Colchester (by chance during their local carnival week) and which, against all reasonable expectations, lasted well into August, if not slightly later.

31. Pacific locomotive 'Saint Johnstoun'. Peppercorn development of Class A1/1 Pacific (which in turn was a Thomson rebuild of Gresley Pacific Class A10. Tractive effect 37,400 lb. Boiler pressure 250 psi. Cylinders 19 x 26 ins; wheel diameter 80 ins. (Photo: the late James Beveridge, Guardbridge)

An interesting record on 30th July was that of the Hunt Class 'The Cleveland' on a 7.52 p.m. Friday evening train from Perth to Dundee (West) Station, whilst a more usual rostering was that of Class A1 Pacific 'St Johnstoun' on a 5.35 p.m. Sunday evening train from Dundee (Tay Bridge) to Kirkcaldy. These A1/1 class Thompson locomotives became a well recorded feature of Dundee rostering over this period. There was a somewhat abnormal appearance on the same duty, some six weeks later, of an unrecorded A4 Pacific.

A melancholy record is of the last train from Ladybank to Perth behind a Pickersgill 4-4-0. A particularly sombre moment is recalled when the uncoupled engine left its train and headed up the line in a somewhat desolate and muted Perth station, so long remembered as a scene of bustle and activity. But times were changing, and the pace of change accelerating.

The remaining entries relate to travel by the Sunday evening train from Kirkcaldy to Glasgow Queen Street. With the exception of an appearance by 'Wizard of the Moor' on 30th December 1955, Class B1 engines monopolised the duty (including some stalwarts: No. 61118 (twice) and Nos. 61103; 61140; 61146; 61344; also 61262 (an engine which continued to appear across the residual days of steam traction).

Chapter 33

The end of an auld sang

In 1956, the year had barely opened when a sombre note was struck.

The date of closure of the original line from Leuchars to Tayport for the north by train-ferry was announced as 7th January. As my parents had, that year, extended their New Year holiday for a few days, and in so doing abandoned a practice of many years, I decided that I would have an additional few days also, and make a sentimental, final journey on the 7th.

Queen Street Station was therefore left on the evening of Friday 6th and the familiar 7.37 p.m. train joined, as so often in years past. The engine in this case was 'Stirlingshire'. On the following evening I boarded the 7.26 p.m. at Kirkcaldy for Leuchars, behind Gresley A4 Pacific 'William Whitelaw'. This recalled its namesake, built in Hyde Park works in 1925 and later renamed.

There were few at Leuchars, though the Tayport Provost, his wife and a tiny group of companions had gathered to join the last train. The night was one of high wind, of the strident variety which can so often scour that area at such seasons. In the unmodified waiting room as it still remained, a coal fire burned in the cast-iron grate. One thought of Dean of Guild W.T. Linskill stepping off the ill-fated train on the evening of 28th December 1879, though the present building would not have been extant in those days, the original station having been burned down in later years (by suffragettes – so rumour had it). 'Can scarcely be as bad as '79,' I thought, 'but no doubt with some of its features.'

The atmosphere in the waiting room was gloomy, likewise, and there was no general discussion.

In a short time the bark of the train was heard from the direction of the Motray confluence and a morose band trouped out on to the exposed platform. Through the stone overbridge at the south end she nosed her way and, appropriately perhaps, the engine was identified as a Scott. As she drew forward her name was deciphered as an old familiar denizen of these parts, 'Jingling Geordie', an engine recalled vividly from many a journey. But she was a survivor, this engine, for it was she who on 3rd January forty-nine years before had collided, tender-first, with the NBR Atlantic 'Dunedin' at Queensferry Junction, when coming off a branch now obliterated by the M8.

Station duties were brief and soon completed, and we drew

32. Scott Class 'Jingling Geordie' just after nationalisation. At Thornton Junction, possibly just before taking the Dundee train via the coast. Built Cowlairs, October 1914; withdrawn January 1957. (Photo: Author, 27.8.49)

forward up the familiar branch towards Leuchars Old, at whose signal box the tablet was uplifted. All those years of childhood travel surged back, in vivid memories. To me this was more than simply the lopping off of an insignificant, redundant, non-earning branch. To me it was a significant milestone which marked the final abandonment of old time-worn ways and the approach of a future that could hold many a challenge.

We passed over the crossing and headed up that long straight beyond, with the ancient castle mound to our left which had seen eight centuries of change and decay. To our right was the long stand of noble trees that I had so admired as a boy. The wind was, as ever, blowing from the west and bending their tops towards the moorland.

The engine was making some dark smoke now, the fireman possibly preparing for his task beyond Tayport, and possibly making good if there had been a stormy ascent of Stravithie Bank. This smoke was wind-driven towards the tops, contrasting dramatically with the lighter high-vaulted sky above them. I shall not readily forget that scene, symbolic, perhaps, of a time for increasing care to displace memories of much undiluted pleasure.

As always came that moment of wonder as, after shaking off the forest proper, we veered to the left and on our right appeared, of a sudden, all the twinkling lights of the estuary and the fringes of the Angus Coast. But now it was down to earth again as we threaded the dimly lit approaches to the town and the dark regions of the sawmill and its spreading yards (which, though we knew it not, was, like so much else, eventually to vanish completely from the scene). Slowly we steamed into the platform. A lone piper was there and a modest assembly of townspeople.

I did not wish to be first off: that was the prerogative of the Provost, his friends and fellow townsmen. But I had divined aright. The fireman had done his job well. No sooner had we stopped than the 'safeties' lifted, giving the piper a stern challenge.

In the gloom of the station entrance, I made out the figures of my father and his brother from Glasgow. I moved toward them and, as of old, we headed up Dalgleish Street where but a few years back had stood these little houses of fishermen, mussel-dredgers and sailors – whalers, some of them.

Few words were spoken. Our thoughts, I believe, were as one, in a situation which for us was deeply symbolic.

As we walked up that slightly inclined way, just as in those many days of yesterday, there came the rumble of the train behind the old ice house and, immediately thereafter, a deepening bark, as she tackled that stern bank through the rock-cutting ahead, unremitting past the two 'lights' and the dark Serpentine Wood.

Back from the rock face came the sturdy echo as 'Jingling Geordie' sounded her farewell drum-beat. If ever there was an age of innocence, then, it had gone.

Only one Tayport New Year was to follow. My aunt, whose house it had been, had died on the first day of 1955. By the next New Year, that of 1957, my Glasgow-resident uncle would be gone. My father would follow him barely a week after the following New Year of 1958 and shortly after that, my mother and my other aunt would leave Fife.

All these events lay some time ahead; but the mould had cracked in 1955 and that event of early 1956 seemed, thereafter, like a marker point in time. It was as if some of the darkness that was to follow seemed, somehow, to have been felt in premonition.

If?

To the railway authorities, the closure of the direct Tayport line no doubt seemed sensible in the short term. Receipts were no doubt meagre, but one wonders if any radical thought had been given to alternative solutions or to the improved prospects that new technology might bring. From a freight aspect the alternative link from Dundee did not seem a rational option and though minor movements did continue for a little time, business soon withered.

Perhaps that was only a small fraction of a nation-wide malaise. Providing viable competition in the freight field, having regard to the small scale nature of the local traffic, would have been difficult and increasingly so, as time went on. On the passenger side, assuming the utilisation of diesel trains, I have always been of the opinion that the line potential could have been exploited.

St Andrews had potential for traffic. University and school traffic was there for the taking in those days and golf and holiday traffic could have been developed then before the private car had grabbed such traffic for the ensuing two decades. The once-heavy commuter traffic to Dundee from Tayport could have been developed especially in years to come, although demands for another halt at the south-east end of the town would have had to be accommodated: a much easier proposition operationally with diesel multiple units.

Across the Tay, there was still a nucleus of traffic to the commuter towns of West Ferry, Broughty Ferry, Monifeith and Carnoustie. My thesis was that a diesel service could have been devised to exploit, in a combined service, the potential of St Andrews, Tayport, the Newports, Wormit as well as Broughty, Monifeith and even Arbroath. A shuttle-type service between St Andrews and Arbroath could have catered for all these communities with one set of stock, leaving the main line to handle express passengers and long-distance freight.

It was not to be known then that the siting of the Old Course Hotel would sterilise the St Andrews track and traffic. Nor was it visualised that the Tay Road Bridge would strangle, for ever, any such scheme completely, if capital could not be found for a bridge over the southern approach road. Perhaps the Railway Authorities were aware of such potential developments and were more prescient than they were given credit for. Perhaps they foresaw the all-conquering power of the private car: the politically invincible road-lobby and planning authorities universally endowed with a 'road-only' solution to any transport situation.

If so, then perhaps their decision was inevitable. Forty years later, however, one might have second thoughts.

With hindsight and the ultimate arrival of a rationally researched transport policy, a 'circular' modern transport system could be attractive, provided that, prior to acceptance, the Tay Rail Bridge has not suffered traffic rationing from years of economic stringency. Strands that once were straight are now hopelessly intertwined. New motive-power, new technology, new politics and a new race of men have all arrived. Much water has flowed under the bridge.

Perhaps we should abjure past conjecture and face up to the problem of tomorrow.

Chapter 34

1956 journeys; 'Madras' in immaculate condition at Bedford; A3 Pacific 'Spearmint'; Norman MacKillop's engine; renewal work on Forth Bridge soleplates

One notable English (work-related) sighting is recorded in the 1956 notes. This related to a journey from Bedford to London on 28th October, when I travelled behind 5XP, Jubilee Class No. 5575, 'Madras' in immaculate and spotless condition, with the 8.36 from that town. This class was designed by Stanier in 1934 and had a tractive effort of 26,610 lb.

For a period, starting in May, I had to make regular Sunday afternoon visits to Edinburgh to visit my mother in hospital and this I did, utilising a train around 2.00 p.m. from Queen Street low level station via Bathgate and returning from Waverley via Falkirk, with the 6.40 p.m. ex Waverley. I recorded a number of the return journeys.

Two of these the trains were double-headed. So, on 9th September we had, up front, B1 'Sir Alexander Erskine' coupled to B1 No. 61340.

On 19th September we travelled behind B1 No. 61007 coupled to Director 'Lord Glenallan'. While on the other of these trains we had a single B1 locomotive.

On 20th January 1957, 'Union of South Africa' was noted on the main line.

Some journeys were also made from Kirkcaldy to Waverley and the locomotives noted were: A3 Pacific 'Spearmint' on 2nd September, and a Gresley VI 2-6-2 tank on the 7.17 p.m. on 9th September.

B1s Nos. 61119, 61113, 61166 and 63014 and 61244 ('Strang Steel') provided motive power on certain other afternoons.

Several Sunday evening trips were made on the 'old faithful' train from Kirkcaldy to Glasgow. All those journeys were made behind B1 locomotives (of numbers: 61146, 61402, 61342, 61197, 61133, 61166, 61244, 63014, 61342, 61344 and 61243 ('Sir Harold Mitchell'). At least two of these journeys were extremely interesting, as the train was routed by Dunfermline, Alloa and the Little Forth (steam-operated swing-) bridge (now demolished), Larbert and Greenhill.

This was to facilitate Sunday work on the Forth Bridge, involving the renewal of sole plates on the approach spans of the bridge and, to my mind, illustrating the versatility and professionalism that was demonstrated by the railway engineers and seldom acknowledged.

There was one recording of a trip from Dundee with the 6.05 p.m. to Thornton on 12th August behind Gresley Class V2 (No. 60885), an ubiquitous and most effective class of engines used frequently on the main line through Kirkcaldy in my early days.

An early B1, 'Klipspringer', was the engine on the 6.40 p.m. from Waverley to Queen Street on 20th May.

Of interest was the appearance of 'Glen Beasdale' on the 5.35 p.m. from Tayport to Dundee on 19th June, a return to one of its old haunts.

On the Buchanan Street to Dundee route, some sightings were recorded of type B1 and Class 5 locomotives, including on 22nd April 1957 a Caprotti Class 5 (73124) and on 4th May 1957 a Standard Class 5 (73124).

CHAPTER 35

1957–9 events: first sampling of a Swindon-designed train-set; 'Edie Ochiltree' on the Aberdeen Express; a stowaway behind Caley 123; a multiplicity of Class 5 locomotives on the Caley main line from Dundee to Glasgow (Buchanan Street)

By the end of 1957, the signs of change were becoming marked.

On 20th October of that year I recorded a journey on a Western Region designed diesel-train between Edinburgh (Haymarket) and Glasgow (Queen Street). In contrast, I noted 'Simon Glover' heading my 8.41 p.m. train from Inverkeithing to Kirkcaldy.

Interestingly, I travelled on the 8.04 from Waverley to Kirkcaldy on 20th June 1958 behind 'Glen Quoich', which was shunted to allow the London to Aberdeen train to pass. When this appeared, it was drawn by the Director Class loco 'Edie Ochiltree'. The old brigade seemed to be determined to hang on to the last.

On 5th September, the B1 Class loco 'Sir Alexander Erskine Hill' took me from Dundee to Tayport, but on 5th October, that day's train had a diesel multiple unit train providing the service.

In August, I twice made the 6.05 p.m. journey from Dundee (Tay Bridge) to Thornton behind a Pacific: A2/1 Class (No. 60509 'Waverley' on the 10th; A3 Class No. 60099 and 'Call Boy' – of many a nostalgic memory – on the 17th).

The most fascinating trip for many a long day occurred on Saturday 16th October 1958. I had spent a somewhat gruelling day at Tayport attempting to return my aunt's garden to a condition approximating to its former impressive order. I left Tayport behind a B1, in threatening weather conditions, and at Dundee took the 7.10 p.m. Class 5 hauled train to Perth. There I had hoped to transfer to the Glasgow express, ex Aberdeen. The weather had assumed storm conditions, however, and this may have delayed the connection which was running considerably late. As I awaited its arrival, I observed Caley 123 at the head of a pair of vintage coaches taking water. I gathered from its passengers that it was bound for Glasgow. As there was no positive information about the 'ex-Aberdeen', I decided to stow away on 123's train, as there was accommodation aboard. The storm became quite intense and there was some delay at Greenloaning and Kinbuck, but 123 stormed on resolutely, and we steamed into Buchanan Street Station at 10.35 p.m..

Nine journeys were made in the course of that year on the Sunday evening train between Thornton and Glasgow and with

33. 'Caley 123' returns to Hyde Park, the scene of its birth. Built in 1886 at Hyde Park works for Edinburgh Exhibition. With 4 bogie coaches it ran 100.75 m in 107.75 minutes as a daily average on the line between Carlisle and Edinburgh on racing days. (Photo: official NBL photographer; obtained in NBL employment)

one exception the motive power provided was by a B1 Class locomotive (specifically Nos. 61277, 61118, 61073, 61099 and 61219 amongst the performers). The exception was a Class 5 (44980), and that trip behind her was made in a very severe thunderstorm, which made viewing from the Forth Bridge quite spectacular.

Class 5 engines were the performers on the Buchanan Street to Dundee West route: Recorded motive power provision was thus: Standard Class 5 on 19th April 1958; Caprotti Class 5s on 24th July, 5th September and 3rd October; 44768 Caprotti 5 on 24th August. Further Class 5s were observed on: 6th September (10.00 p.m. ex Dundee) and 5th October (3.00 p.m. ex Dundee).

A Standard Class 5 was noted on 4th January 1959 (12.05 p.m. ex Perth on the Aberdeen to Glasgow train).

A rather different journey recording, on 5th September 1958, was of a 2-6-4 tank on a Perth to Dundee train.

CHAPTER 36

1959–60: Pacifics reappear; a nostalgic 'last steam' call at Crianlarich; Glasgow to Bothwell Castle and Torrance in the company of the famous; sundry records of locomotive appearances

During 1959 and 1960 there was a reappearance of Pacifics in my notes (which, as have been explained earlier, are of limited observations and not necessarily representative of general practice during the period in question). Thus, Class A2 Peppercorn designed No. 60535, 'Hornet's Beauty' was the locomotive heading the 7.27 p.m. train on which I travelled from Falkirk (High) to Queen Street on 18th March 1961.

Sister engine No. 60528, 'Sun Chariot', was the motive power provided on the 8.42 p.m. Larbert to Buchanan Street train on 15th April 1961.

Again, Class A1 'Bonnie Dundee' 60157 was noted at Inverkeithing on Saturday 10th June 1960, whilst, on Saturday 9th September 1961, on an exploratory visit, we took the 2.36 p.m. train to Galashiels from Edinburgh (Waverley) and found that it was drawn by Class A3-60101 'Cicero'. In the late afternoon, we returned with the 5.41 p.m., and our engine for the journey to Edinburgh was No. 60100 A3 Class 'Spearmint' (so often the subject of articles by Norman Mackillop in his incomparable *Locomotive Express* and elsewhere). Returning that evening to Queen Street from Waverley, A4 Class Pacific No. 60027 'Merlin' provided the motive power. That evening, however, I espied Deltic D900 at Waverley as a very positive sign of changing times.

The opportunity to travel with two organised excursions was

taken during this period. The first expedition was on 30th April and was organised by the Stephenson Locomotive Society. It took the form of a special train drawn by 'Glen Douglas', and the itinerary explored many of the lesser-known branches in Glasgow and adjacent Lanarkshire. The starting point was Hyndland and we travelled by the now electrified suburban line to Haghill and thence via Barnhill and Springburn to Garngaber Junction, where we joined the venerable Monkland and Kirkintilloch route via Bridgend to Coatbridge.

From there we went on via Shettleston to Bothwell (where I recall the massive bing of Bothwell Castle colliery beside the Clyde). We then retraced our path via Haghill to reach Maryhill, where we steamed out on the Kelvin Valley branch, past Summerston with its gaunt colliery and over the bowstring girder bridge spanning the Kelvin to reach Torrance of Campsie. Returning, we went on to Anniesland and thence to Dalmuir and Westerton.

Not a few well-known exponents of locomotive matters were passengers on that excursion and I knew well their reputation. James Aird, with whom I made contact at work, was there, I remember, and I certainly recall the presence of David L. Smith, whose writings I had read with intense interest and admiration and to whose short talk on the old 'Soo West' I had listened, with wrapt attention, in the Mitchell Library several years before.

A much older acquaintance of my youth had read aloud to me Mr Smith's incomparable contribution to the *Railway Magazine*: 'Glasgow and South Western Nights Entertainment' (around January 1938 I estimate) and it had done much to inspire even greater enthusiasm for the world of the railway and the locomotive.

On 17th June 1961, I took my young son with me on an excursion (2.50 p.m. from Queen Street) which was advertised as 'The last K2 excursion to Crianlarich'. Alas, the weather was poor and everyone was totally drenched at Crianlarich, where sustained shelter was, in effect, nil. For my own part, that gave

34. LNER A4 Class Pacific 'Merlin' at Haymarket shed. (Photo D.S. Currie)

me little concern; but my son caught a chill, the results of which, sadly, persisted for some years and caused us great concern. This rather diminished the joy of seeing the Gresley engine in steam on her own heath, as it were. 'Loch Arkaig' it was; and she was well scrutinised (and photographed also), as I note from a book in my possession which, on discovery, gave great pleasure.

Poor Tubby Warren was there, complete with his usual massive collection of equipment (photographic as well as life-sustaining). He greeted me as a 'fellow Hyde Park man of old acquaintance' and spoke to my son of our mutual appearances in that dear old place. Eventually we made our way to Crianlarich lower, on the Callander and Oban line, first noticed in the family peregrinations of summer 1939, as described earlier. All around, the rain continued to drench the peaks and no doubt swell the rivers.

Our homeward journey was symbolic of that era of change, as

the train from Oban arrived hauled by twin NBL diesels – NBL order L94. On the train I was greeted heartily by an NBL man from Atlas Works (Donald Glass – if the memory is authentic). He and his companion had been fishing and had been reasonably successful. It is an ill wind that blows no one any good. The open-third coaches were well crowded, but spirits were high, as they inevitably are on such excursions.

On the 29th of that month, work had taken me to Manchester and I had travelled with the 10.30 p.m. from Glasgow Central to Manchester behind ex LMS Patriot Class 'Sir Frederick Harrison' – an interesting sighting.

Sadly, on 27th May I had to attend a funeral in Newburgh which, in effect, terminated any residential visits to that charming and scenic town. On the journey back, the route taken was by Glen Farg, Devonside and Alloa, so often followed by Jock, my late fellow lodger (of the latter forties). Such was my first and last journey over that route, though, alas, I was in no mood to absorb its beauty. Of the locomotive I made a passing note. No Scott, then, as Jock would have known, but B1 No. 61140.

The residue of the year's recordings fall into the two major observed routes, viz: Thornton and associated locations to Glasgow (Queen Street), and Dundee (West) to Glasgow (Buchanan Street). On the former, my familiar Sunday evening train, of many a journey, was the object of study and on this the B1 Class retained all but sole possession, with all the familiar performers: Nos. 61355, 61263, 61343, 61148, 61180, 61133, 61134 and 61330. This last was built by NBL in 1948 and was withdrawn in 1963. Even for her time was running out!

On the Caley line, the Class 5s all but reigned supreme. Caprottis were much in evidence on 9th August and 14th August 1959. On 28th October 1961 No. 63145 was positively recorded. Miscellaneous Class 5s were noted on 19th September 1962, 12th December 1959 and 19th May 1961.

The balance of recorded turns were covered by: (1) twin-diesels D6134 and D612 on 13th December 1960, heading the 7.15 Buchanan St to Dundee (West) train. (2) V2 Class No. 60822 on 3rd April 1961, and (3) by twin NBL diesels on 1st March 1961 heading the 9.15 Saturdays only Buchanan St to Dundee (West) duty.

Chapter 37

Thornton veterans/Hurricane Thomson and Tony Gray; an unfortunate ex Beardmore apprentice; a first experience behind the 'Austerity'; and the incomparable Toram Beg and the Locomotive Express

After travelling regularly between Fife and Glasgow over a period of some sixteen years, it was inevitable that one grew to recognise the engine men handling these duties. Across the years one might succeed in passing a few words to a fireman here or a driver there, but, generally, one did not get to learn their names. It was of great interest, therefore, many years later, when the shed at Thornton was being closed and many retirals taking place, that a photograph appeared in the local press relating to the retiral function. There were shown many of that hardy band and after such a period of anonymity it was a pleasure to learn their names and to discover that so many were entering into what, one hoped, was a happy retirement after all these years of faithful service. Many a tale they must have had to tell.

Only once on these travels did I see the driver who, with the sanction of the shedmaster, had taken me down to Culross with the breakdown crane to lift marine shafting in 1945 (of which I have recorded details elsewhere). My leavetaking interchange was, of obvious necessity, brief and I was never able to thank him for an unforgettable experience. How many interesting and capable men there are, whom one has encountered on the way, and with whom one would like to yarn yet again; but time has swept on and such opportunities seem so often unattainable.

Sometimes footplatemen, for a variety of reasons, would have to travel back 'on the cushions' after a trip. It was in this way that I met the unforgettable 'Hurricane' Thomson, who earned his nickname when making up time on a (Beattie's) bread train from Glasgow to Fife. A signalman who saw the train passing described the apparition as a hurricane and the driver's nickname was there and then earned. He and his mate were a friendly pair and it was a real pleasure to yarn to them. What a bunch of worthies these railway men were!

35. Shunting at Burntisland, Autumn 1949. Driver Tony Gray. LNER J83 Class of Holmes – NBR design. Built by Nielson, Reid & Co. Ltd., March 1901; withdrawn October 1962. Tractive effort 17,744 lb. (Photo: Author, 22.10.49)

One driver seemed to be most apprehensive when picking up the guard's right-away signal, as his eyes seemed to trouble him. He disappeared from the Glasgow turns for a time. I found him in charge of a J83 shunting engine at Burntisland Docks one Saturday, and after an interesting yarn with him and his fireman, I photographed his engine and got George Ellis to develop and print the shot for me as he gladly did – and then added one more print to his vast collection of ex-NBR engines (and a multitude from other railways). It pleased me not a little that an expert in such matters would consider it worth while to do so.

Many an interesting blether I had with engine men. One exchange which sticks in the mind arose at Dundee on an autumn Saturday evening around 1945, when travelling on the Thornton train. The engine was 'Glen Orchy' and I was invited on to the footplate, as departure was awaited. The fireman told me that he had commenced his apprenticeship with Beardmore's when they were building locomotives (at Dalmuir I believe). When this activity was given up, most of the men were paid off and his apprenticeship was broken. He had found it impossible to find any alternative employer willing to take him on to allow completion of his apprenticeship. In consequence he had had to take rail service as the only option. We had a most interesting talk, and I was sad when I had to make rapid tracks for my carriage.

Another journey is recalled on that same train around the same time of year, when I encountered my first 2-8-0 Austerity locomotive on a train in which I was a passenger. My particular

36. 2-8-0 austerity locomotive at Tayport South box level crossing with a south bound freight or trip working. (Photo: Author, c. early 1950s)

memory is of viewing the unfamiliar and unconventional engine from the rear of its train as it snaked round the slightly sinuous track before St Fort Junction, these undulating hills of grass-covered sand and gravel deposited aeons ago as glacial detritus – now seemingly slipping past in the moonlight.

It was in the very late 1940s that I was introduced to Toram Beg's *Locomotive Express* and thereafter read it monthly from cover to cover. This introduced awareness of the great band of footplatemen then at Haymarket Shed and I read with great pleasure his 'Enginemen Elite'. The *Loco Express* journals induced, if such were possible, an intensification of interest in locomotive operation and those involved in that operation. Each copy was religiously kept and eventually some were bound. How times change! Such is the thought, when one opens copy No. 1 of January 1947. What enthusiasm and hope there then was in that great industry.

Changing trains one evening, at Taybridge Station, Dundee, I got into conversation with a driver, who was waiting to take out the Edinburgh train with a Gresley Pacific. I introduced the subject of the *Locomotive Express* and certain articles were discussed. I asked him whether he knew one driver whose name cropped up frequently in the magazine and he answered in the affirmative. On reflection, I had a growing suspicion that I had spoken to the man in person.

It was around 1953 when I had the pleasure of meeting Toram Beg himself, when the possibility of contributing an article was discussed. He was a thorough gentleman; and it was a delight to speak with him. Often, thereafter, I was able to obtain the Scottish Edition of the *British Railways Magazine* of which he was then editor, and I read his excellent editorials and other informative articles with abiding pleasure.

CHAPTER 38

Continuing footplate aspirations; on a Mauritius locomotive to Princes Street; a rain-drenched Breich and impressions of Lesmahago junction

The quest to travel on a footplate was a lengthy one, with hopes high and attainment long-deferred. Positive progress came only with the period of experience at Thornton Shed, an achievement which continues to be ranked in the miracle category. To have penetrated the offices and inner sanctum of Mr E.D. Trask, Locomotive Running Superintendent – Scottish Region, seemed in itself no mean breakthrough. Finally to stand in the cab of 'Helen Macgregor' and, later, travel on a J37 was a superb consummation after much longing, great research into routes of attack and many a hope deferred.

Yet, the addiction did not then wither. Indeed the desire for further conquest waxed greater. Every approach was contemplated.

The authorised WPR journey to Methil on the footplate of the Big Barclay Tank was a further, though lesser achievement. Even the short spell on the WPR 'Austerity' Saddle Tank from rain-drenched Chemiss Wood to Scott's Road was a moment of achievement, as was the trip on a sister engine down to the Michael Colliery.

Possibly the next authorised experience of great note came some years later, in the fifties. At that time, NBL built two diesel-hydraulic locomotives for the Mauritius Government Railways, which were constructed to standard 4 ft. 8½ ins. gauge and in which I had had a part at the project tendering stage. On their completion, as well as a gradient test on the Thrashbush Incline, full-scale tests were arranged on British Railways tracks and one of the selected routes was from Glasgow Central to Edinburgh Princes St. Much publicity was given to this trial, as it was an excellent opportunity for the company to demonstrate its products to the railway industry. It was duly covered by the press and there appeared a now well-known photograph of the coupled pair standing at the east side of Glasgow Central Station.

A small number of drawing office personnel were selected to

37. About to travel with Mauritius locos to Edinburgh. From left: Author; William Hardie (dec); Kurt Buerkel (dec); 'Gus' Munro; J. Donnelly. (Photo: NBL photographer)

accompany the locomotive on its trial run, and I was one of the fortunate persons chosen. We joined the locomotives (which ran in tandem) at Glasgow Central and returned to that point. At Princes Street, a splendid lunch was provided for invited guests and, again, I was fortunate in being selected to join that group.

Unfortunately, the day dawned intensely wet, and there was much rain on both journeys. A recollection of the intensity of the downpour relates to the return journey, at the point of passing Breich.

An enormous shale bing was alongside and dwarfing all else.

38. Two Mauritius Government Railways diesel-hydraulic locomotives on test on British Railways between Glasgow (Central) Station and Edinburgh (Princes St.) Station – at Glasgow Central. Max tractive effort: low speed range – 35,800 lb. per loco; high speed range – 23,000 lb. per loco. (Photo: given to author by NBL official photographer)

As we headed west the torrents were descending on this bleak vision. All that met the eye was rain, mist or spent shale. Not exactly inspiration for an 'Old Master'.

A feature of that journey was the sensation of being so close to the track. On the return trip, we were running cab-first with the engine-compartment between us and the second loco. There was, therefore, no projection ahead of us, as in most modern nose-constructed locomotives. The track layout at junctions such as Motherwell seemed to fly threateningly up towards one at speed, in something of the same manner as steel sections do when viewed from the inspection bridge of a steel rolling mill, where one has the momentary illusion that the rolled sections are speeding straight towards one's eyes.

The test run was an excellent opportunity to study design

39. LMS 'up' 'Royal Scot', passing Bridge Street, Glasgow. (Photo D.S. Currie)

requirements for such locomotives and, not least, to observe the actions and responses of the hydraulic transmission and to correlate these to the nature of the route, gradient variations in particular.

None of the romance of the steam footplate was there, perhaps, but there were the technical and engineering affiliations of any rail journey. Noticeable on that journey was the diminished role of the driver. The fascination of steam operation lies in the skill demonstrated by the driver in his selection of throttle setting and cut-off as he adjusts engine performance to the needs of the 'road' and all the other salient variables, as they change from point to point, along the way. Demanding, too, is the fireman's task as he controls boiler output in anticipation of engine demands. There lies the major interest: in watching a skilled partnership control their engine to meet not only timetable and safety demands, but also to exercise stringent economy in the use of steam (fuel) and water.

CHAPTER 39

To Aberdeen on the footplate of a Black 5 and home likewise by way of the 'West Coast Postal' and a 'burning deck'

To travel on a diesel-hydraulic locomotive was, however, easily achieved. In the Atlas works, a shunter of this type was employed, where it had taken over from the venerable steam crane locomotive, which had served the Atlas and especially the Marne flanging shop so well for so many years. At lunch times I would head there (if no other works area was scheduled for attention) and the driver would, inevitably, invite me aboard. It was a slightly 'rocky road', but it was a wide yard with much scope for travel and, on occasion, the opportunity to try one's hand.

The most momentous advance took place in October 1954 when I received a letter with the magic words: 'I have much pleasure in sending you herewith a Footplate Permit No. . . . . . . to enable you to travel on the footplate of the locomotive working the 10.00 a.m. train from Glasgow to Aberdeen on the 16th October 1954.'

This was signed by the Assistant Motive Power Superintendent at 302 Buchanan Street, Glasgow. Having decided that only a direct approach would produce results, I had indeed apprehensively approached the Joint Managing Director of NB Loco Co., Mr R. Arbuthnott, who was on the council of the Institution of Locomotive Engineers, indicating my desire to have footplate experience. He in turn, had referred the matter to Mr C.R. Campbell, the Motive Power Superintendent, with the happy result described above.

In good time, I joined Perth driver Arthur Adams on the footplate of a Class 5 locomotive at Buchanan Street Station. Mr Adams told me that he normally shared a Standard Class 5 engine with a fellow driver, which was certainly a desirable practice at Perth Shed for some time.

After all these years of waiting, one no doubt would expect a detailed record of the first authorised main-line footplate journey, and certainly intentions were of the best when we set out. To achieve this result was (as I rapidly found out) not as simple as I had expected it to be (influenced by much reading of the works of such masters of their profession as Cecil J. Allen, O.S. Nock and others). My major obsession was avoidance of any intrusion on the work of the driver and fireman. This interfered with accurate noting of regulator and cut-off positions, if one was simultaneously keeping tabs on exact locations and their exact mileage. Wandering to and fro in the cab would certainly not assist the fireman, especially if one's legs had not acclimatised to a footplate in motion.

The locomotive, I was told, was just out of the shops and so should have been 'in good nick'. The riding seemed normally good, but a little rough at low cut offs (though, owing to lack of experience, any such comments are possibly valueless). Weather on the journey was good.

The load is recalled as twelve bogies and somehow or other I estimated the load at 385 tons, although that is possibly a suspect figure, and there is no way of checking figures now, forty years later. The limited notes which I did jot down have not withstood a whole series of moves between locations, houses and containers within them, and the scrap of paper remaining cannot, frustratingly, be translated in any rational way. I feel that it is incumbent, however, to give some rational data on such a long-awaited event rather than ignore it completely, but the reader must not attempt any deep or meaningful analysis therefrom.

Had there been any attempt at record time-keeping, as of course there was none, then it would have received an early setback. We lost ten minutes having the train checked at Madgecroft Box, as the preceding signalman had reported a carriage door swinging open. There was, also, a permanent way slowing in Castlecary Glen. Water was taken at Stirling, I recall. The coal was described as 'poor'; and was a mixture of poor coal briquettes and dross but the reason for this (hopefully) unusual circumstance, I cannot now recall.

The fireman seemed to use only one injector throughout and I was told that this was the exhaust injector. I was surprised that the firedoor seemed to be left open for a substantial portion of the time.

From the hieroglyphics of forty years ago it would appear that Larbert was passed at $10.45^1/_2$ a.m. and Alloa Junction at $10.48^1/_2$ a.m. but these blurred figures are no doubt of little value. According to these smudges, Madgecroft, 11.4 miles from Buchanan Street, had been left at 10.30 a.m. and Castlecary Box, some 16.5 miles from Glasgow, passed at 10.40 a.m.. From the scribbles, it could be interpreted that the throttle was eased back to meet local restrictions as follows: to one half at St Rollox; to seven-eighths at Robroyston; to seven-eighths at Cumbernauld; to one half for Castlecary Glen pw restriction; to one quarter at Carmuirs West and Larbert Junctions; and to three quarters at Alloa Junction but the document is so defaced and erased it is possibly pointless even to attempt any comment, and unfair to Driver Adams. The cut-off figures have vanished, alas, completely.

The miraculously surviving scrap of paper implies that I had set down in advance the main locations on the route, and, I suspect, the timetable timings for these locations with the objective of setting alongside the actual timings. On the second lap of the journey, these sets of figures may have been interchanged though I suspect not.

If these recordings are correct, timings were: Coupar Angus 12.01 p.m.; Forfar 12.22 p.m.; Bridge of Dun 12.43 p.m.; Laurencekirk 1.03 p.m.; Fordoun 1.10 p.m.; Stonehaven

1.25 p.m. and Ferryhill 1.50 p.m. My records imply a timing of eighteen minutes from Gleneagles to Perth but how accurately this was taken with a wrist watch who now can tell? This distance is, I believe, 15.75 miles, implying a 52.5 m.p.h. average speed over that largely downhill section but which also includes Moncreiff Tunnel and the Perth station approaches.

Mr Adams told me that he normally shared a Standard Class 5 on a regular basis with his mate but the engine on which I travelled, nonetheless, was a Perth engine. At Perth, there was a change of crew but their names have vanished. As ever, they were a most friendly pair.

At Forfar, which was on a curved section of track, there was a tendency to slip at starting and sanding was applied. A heavy fire was put on at Perth and there was frequent firing to Stonehaven. Throttle opening was mostly around half, it is recalled. There was considerable traffic on that Saturday afternoon journey; and platforms at the long-closed stations at Laurencekirk, Fordoun and Drumlithie are particularly recalled in this connection.

The driver became quite annoyed about this, as the passengers inevitably crowded to the back of the train, thus involving him in some double stops which implied the loss of precious minutes. The cliff-side running toward Cove Bay was, as ever, impressive and the long run down to Ferryhills Junction and Aberdeen terminus with the wonderful approach across the Dee was duly savoured.

At Aberdeen Station, I had a hurried snack and made my way back to travel on the prestigious 'West Coast Postal'. Once again the engine was a Class 5, in this case from Aberdeen Shed. The load was, of course, lighter than that of the morning, being of nine vehicles and estimated (or established) at 285 tons.

The first eight miles to Portlethen were steadily uphill. Beyond Stonehaven, we were climbing again for seven miles to Drumlithie. The fireman reckoned that the tubes were dirty and he made use of a pail of sand in an attempt to effect some cleaning.

Departure from Aberdeen was at 3.30 p.m. and Forfar was reached at 4.36 p.m. implying a coverage of 57.5 miles in 66 minutes and an average speed of 52.1 m.p.h.

At Forfar we took water and whilst the fireman directed the 'bag' into the tender rank, I manipulated the valve at the column. From that moment on, I never forgot that water valves are invariably left-handed.

Forfar was left at 4.39 p.m., three minutes after arrival, and Perth was reached at 5.12 p.m. During the journey we had some fine spirited running and I only regret that I had not had the ability to record some of the actual speeds achieved.

Writing this in 1994, I have picked from my shelves an old favourite volume by O.S. Nock and I note therein a log of the same train, some time prior to 1950, and he records a timing of 68 minutes 13 seconds to Forfar with 345 tons, so my figures for that section of the journey may well stand analysis. Presentation of my results should have been done in 1954, not 1994, but that has been the story of my life: the invariable lack of sufficient time to do everything that one would wish to do, and seldom to achieve – except in scheduled work – the high standard of completion which one would wish.

At Perth I had to bid farewell to my new-found comrades as they were bound for the south via Mossend. Now I joined the 5.35 p.m. train for Glasgow. Yet again the locomotive was a Class 5 (No. 44977). As I presented my credentials, I received a warm welcome and the invitation: 'Come on the burning deck.' This I did with alacrity. The crew were both Perth men but I have no record of their names.

It was now somewhat dark, as the weather was deteriorating and to my shame, after Moncreiff tunnel, I must admit I could make out nothing and held to the cab side until I could accustom my senses to my moving, noisy environment. A major mistake, of course, was to gaze at the white heat of the fire and vision took some time to normalise. When a sense of direction returned, there was exhilaration in racing down to Dunblane. A further scribble suggests that the five miles from Dunblane to Stirling were covered in seven minutes, implying a speed average of 43 m.p.h. I had reached the conclusion that the locomotive was slightly off-beat and this was more noticeable when she was notched up. On that journey both injectors were used.

40. Former GNSR Tank–LNER Class Z5 at Aberdeen quay in BR days. Built 1915 for shunting at Aberdeen harbour. Scrapped between 1956–66. (Photo: Author, 21.7.51)

After Larbert there were hold ups. At Castlecary Glen we had an adverse signal. This was followed by the pw slack of the morning, which had been identified at Perth on the way up, as having been caused by a broken axle on a guard's van. There were also signal slowings between Garnqueen and Stepps. Arrival was clocked at Buchanan Street as being 7.14$^{1}/_{2}$ p.m.. I was loathe to leave my good companions of 'the burning deck', but made my way to the adjacent Cowcaddens tram stop. On the tram, I thrust my hand into my pocket, which had been in close proximity to the firebox backplate for quite a time. The coin was still very hot. The conductor was obviously amazed when he sensed its temperature. But now it was time for me to cool down from my heady experiences and return to humdrum reality.

CHAPTER 40

To Winton Pier on the Arran boat train

There were other footplate journeys, however, which, I must admit, did not bear the full stamp of authority. The strident impressions of one such trip, in the very late summer of 1950, are lucidly retained. My contact then, had been a senior railway engineer, though not from the locomotive department.

The journey had been to Winton Pier with an Arran boat train and had commenced at St Enoch's station on a dazzling Saturday afternoon. There, I had stepped on to the footplate of a 2-6-4 Tank in immaculate condition, no doubt in the best 'Soo West' tradition.

The driver was a most friendly man who did everything feasibly possible to give me an excellent introduction to that working, comprising the characteristics of the route and the features of the engine, over whose capabilities – especially its economy in water consumption – he enthused. The immediate impression was of a man in total command of his job and proud of his industry and its traditions. His young fireman also proved helpful in the extreme and most companionable. Such men, of whom the railways seemed to have so many, were truly the salt of the earth.

The initial part of the route was over the 'Canal Line', now reopened, I believe, after earlier official vandalism had imposed its demise. Corkerhill, that legendary spot of the GSWR locomotive department after the abandonment of the St Enoch Sheds, was passed; but that was noted after crossing the Clyde and traversing the Gorbals by that route recalled from the journeys of childhood in 1938. In the environs of Paisley the old, over-ambitious and drastically short-lived branch to the Barrhead area, still-born as a result of meteoric tramway car success, was pointed out.

There was much fast running as we steamed smoothly down by Milliken Park, Glengarnock and Dalry to branch to Ardrossan town and terminate at Winton Pier, where a large crowd, obviously enthusiastic and in characteristic relaxed and joyful holiday mood, disgorged to join the steamer (which, if memory be trusted, was the old twin-screw, turbine steamer *Marchioness of Graham*). Odd, it seemed, to scan the crowd from the footplate and not the footplate from the crowd.

The happy throng duly detrained, the coaches were detached and off to Ardrossan shed we went. There we had some time to spend before the next task. I was duly taken round the shed and at one point taken onto the footplate of a Caley 0-6-0 locomotive and had an exposition of all its salient features and footplate fittings.

Some discussion on locomotive matters followed, with specific references to 'Soo West' engines and men, in both of which, I was intensely interested, the works of David L. Smith having made me a total convert.

My uncle, who in his diverse career had worked in Greenock for a time, had told me of Princes Pier and of G&SW journeys from and to that terminus as well as of journeys to reach Northern Ireland during his working time with Harland and Wolff in their Belfast shipyard. All of this, and the historic alliance between the G&SW and the NBR, had made me most interested in the system of the former.

It transpired in the course of our discussion that the shed blacksmith was an uncle of one of my current senior colleagues, who was from a G&SW family and for whom I had the highest regard as a drawing office colleague and draughtsman. That colleague, alas, like so many other excellent and skilled citizens, emigrated not long thereafter – a great loss not only to Glasgow and the West but to the whole of Scotland.

In due course we steamed back to Winton Pier and collected our quota of passengers, Glasgow bound. It was a brilliantly clear evening such as can grace the very start of September. That somewhat flat region embracing the rearward lands of Ardrossan, Stevenston and South Beach may not be described as being high on scenic beauty, but on that evening there was magic abroad and perhaps I saw them through rose-tinted spectacles.

As we steamed towards the junction we scanned to the south from whence came the main line from Stranraer and Ayr. In that quarter, the whole countryside seemed to be bathed in a mellow suffused light and across the bents the lights of an unknown town twinkled alluringly, with that early-evening aura of the romantic and the mysterious.

Off came the signal for the main line and we were away with a 'clean pair of wheels'. A five minute check was encountered up the line at some forgotten location, but we regained a spanking pace and at 7.50 p.m. came to a stand at our destination in the vastness of St Enoch's Station. The exhilaration of that day will resonate for many a day.

So! back to the digs by tram and foot to give landlord Bob (my thoroughly practical and long-experienced mentor on all footplate matters) a blow by blow account of that never-to-be-forgotten day of the Arran boat train.

Chapter 41

Cowlairs tunnel and two outrageous journeys

Many many times I had travelled by train up Queen Street Tunnel before I had the opportunity to sample the extreme conditions experienced therein by the engine-crew of a steam locomotive. I had frequently discussed this section of line with my landlord Bob, and at an earlier period of existence with Jock, my former fellow-lodger, both of whom had had much practical experience of operating in its murky interior. Bob, in fact, could recall his duties as a fireman in the ancient days of cable-assisted haulage and dismissed the manual unshipping of the coupling in that operation as mere routine, though it conjured up alarming visions for me.

Descriptions, generally, did not sound inviting. I had directed enquiries to Bob concerning one tunnel-runaway which had occurred in the tunnel many years before, of which I had been reading. The account given had implied that at one stage in the precipitate descent, the driver had asked the fireman to go back and sever the vacuum train pipe, an action which to me had seemed to be an impossibly precarious and impracticable action to recommend.

In his inimitable way, Bob had given a virtual treatise on the tunnel and the proper procedures for traversing that incline but, after such a gap of years, it would not only be futile but would probably do injustice to his measured assessment to attempt to recall or report his thesis. His main assertion was, however, that when a train was sliding downhill with no response from the brakes, the necessary action was to throw off the brakes and make a fresh application. Like so many of these discussions, how fervently do I wish that there had been time to record accurately the essential comments.

It was in early spring 1952 before I had the opportunity to sample the tunnel journey for myself and I still feel the guilt of persuading a driver to take me with him (although he must have felt reasonably sure of non detection). The engine was a standard Class Four and the trip all the more novel for that. He drew the line at allowing me to cross the Forth Bridge, no doubt because of the timekeepers at both extremities, who in those days logged the timing of every train crossing the bridge. The tunnel trip was, without question, a stirring experience and yet another not readily forgotten.

The atmosphere was oppressive and for someone such as my late companion, who suffered quite severely from bronchial trouble, must have been quite dire on most occasions. I personally did not find the experience frightening, but the din of the exhaust and the noise of a passing train, together with the inability to see what lay ahead, was a little daunting, as is any situation where one is at an initial stage of not having yet adapted to the unknown or acquired control techniques to deal subsequently with a situation that may seen threatening.

Bob and Jock had always spoken of the tunnel's first and second 'eyes', which earlier I had sought to locate and identify from surface level; but from within, and adapting to a new element, I was not aware of them at all.

The most preposterous footplate journey had been experienced in the early summer of 1950, on the footplate of a B1 class locomotive, of which because of its nature I hesitate to give details, even more than forty years on.

It took place on a major main line close to my native heath but with a non-Fife crew. In fairness to the driver it should be emphasised that he genuinely believed that I was a railway man and I had been introduced as one, though I had made no strenuous attempts to describe myself as such. It was, however, a trip with the maximum of exhilaration and it intensified my desire for more experience of the same. It is to be hoped that the innocent passengers were blissfully unaware of any abnormality in their journey.

I had a further experience that same year when *en route* overnight to Oban. I travelled for several miles on the footplate of a named Black Five and watched, from the engine, the dawn rise over the hills of Argyllshire.

41. Believed to be of Holmes 592 Class of 1886 at Cowlairs shed (replaced by Eastfield running shed in 1904) with R. Fairgrieve as fireman. If this is indeed NBR 592 then she is the engine shown at the Edinburgh International Exhibition (May-Oct. 1886). Driving wheel diameter 7ft.; tractive effort 12,756 lb. (Photo presented to the author by the late Mr R. Fairgrieve)

42. The first day of the non-stop 'Flying Scotsman'. Footplateman prior to departure at Edinburgh Waverley. LH driver and fireman Gateshead men. (Photo: originally property of former Eastfield Shed running foreman R. Fairgrieve, my one-time landlord)

43. Dandy coach at Port Carlisle. In my youth this was on permanent exhibition at Waverley Station, adjacent to platform 19. (Success series postcard, postmarked 4 September 1913)

44. The first steam-hauled train on the Drumburgh–Port Carlisle branch, after withdrawal of the 'Dandy coach'. Driver Herkess on footplate. (Photo presented to author by Driver Herkess's brother-in-law R. Fairgrieve)

45. The 'Northern Belle' on the 'Waverley Road' in prewar days (1933) returning from the Highlands. Gresley K2 and J39 Class locomotives in tandem near Stobs Camp. (Photo: Rudolf Haddon Collection. Given to author by Mr Haddon)

46. Axlebox squad, Hyde Park 1947. From left: Charge hand D. Russell; Wm Gibson; Flo Lynch (Brown); first year apprentice J. Mone; author; driller Abe ?. Large 'boxes' for SAR (last plain bearing boxes). Small box in foreground South American Spore (Brazil?) (Photo: William Brown, squad fitter, early March 1947)

47. Author with fitter William Crainey in front of SAR 15F Class locomotive (L961) steaming in Hyde Park yard. (Photo William Brown, early 1947)

48. Electric adhesion/rack locomotive en route from Lucerne to Interlaken (narrow gauge). (Photo: Author, 9.4.55)

49. An American Mammoth in the Henry Ford museum, Detroit. Seen during a short respite from attendance at a Company Energy Conference and mills visit, Saturday 26th September 1987. 2-6-6-6 by Lima for Chesapeake & Ohio, c.600 tons weight; 125 feet long. (Photo: from a postcard published exclusively for the Edison Institute, Henry Ford Museum and Dearborn village – Dearborn, Michigan)

50. Keith Junction in Scotrail days. A temporary return to locomotive haulage. Locomotive named 'Confederation of British Industry'. (Photo: Author, 19 September 1992)

51. Testing an Ulster Transport hydraulic transmission manufactured by Messrs J.M. Voith GmbH after examination and overhaul after many years of successful service in Ulster. (Simple form of brake necessary to achieve evaluation of stall torque.) Author taking output speed with tachometer on 14.9.55. (Photo: NBL photographer. Obtained 1955 when hydraulic transmission test engineer)

52. Swedish steam locomotive by Nidquist & Holm, Trollhätten, 1947. At Strömstad during a run to mark the 1903 opening of the railway from Uddevalla to Strömstad and Lysekil (Norra Bohusbanan). (Photo: Author, 12.6.93)

Epilogue

Not a few of the foregoing pages were penned at a time when it seemed that the railways – if not of the UK then certainly of Scotland – were hastening to their extinction.

Today, one senses a change of mood.

As we approach the threshold of a new millennium, society recognises environmental problems that potentially darken the path ahead.

Assessment indicates transport as a vital variable in the equation and one to be evaluated while there is yet time.

For the first time in a succession of drear' decades it would seem that the potential of rail is to be acknowledged and utilised, effectively.

Whatever organisational structure the future ultimately holds for rail, its success as an industry throws down an immense challenge to all engineers in any way involved in the creation and maintenance of the railways of the next millennium.

If they grasp this challenge with the same resolution and creativity as did their forerunners of the last two centuries, as they will, then that new railway will rise to capture the enthusiasm and imagination of generations yet to come.